Show me your garden
and I shall tell you what you are.

ALFRED AUSTIN

Includes Gardening Journal

Garden Witchery

Magick from the Ground Up

Ellen Dugan

Llewellyn Publications
Woodbury, Minnesota

FIRST EDITION

Seventh Printing, 2010

Book design and editing by Rebecca Zins
Cover design and interior zone map by Gavin Dayton Duffy
Cover statue photograph © 2002 Jonathan Nutt / gardenImage
Cover ivy photograph © 2002 Photodisc
Illustrations © Kerigwen

LIBRARY OF CONGRESS CATALOGING-IN-PUBLICATION DATA

Dugan, Ellen, 1963-
    Garden witchery : magick from the ground up / Ellen Dugan.
        p. cm.
    Includes bibliographical references and index.
    ISBN 13: 978-0-7387-0318-3
    ISBN 10: 0-7387-0318-4
    1. Magic. 2. Gardens—Miscellanea. 3. Gardening—Miscellanea. 4. Witchcraft. I. Title.

BF1623.G37 D84 2003

133.4'3—dc21

2002038933

Llewellyn Worldwide does not participate in, endorse, or have any authority or responsibility concerning private business transactions between our authors and the public.

All mail addressed to the author is forwarded but the publisher cannot, unless specifically instructed by the author, give out an address or phone number.

Any Internet references contained in this work are current at publication time, but the publisher cannot guarantee that a specific location will continue to be maintained. Please refer to the publisher's website for links to authors' websites and other sources.

Llewellyn Publications
A Division of Llewellyn Worldwide Ltd.
2143 Wooddale Drive
Woodbury MN 55125-2989
www.llewellyn.com
Llewellyn is a registered trademark of Llewellyn Worldwide Ltd.

Printed in the United States of America

This book is dedicated in loving memory to my grandmother,
Dorothy Catherine
1908-2001
She made a wicked pot roast and was a wonderful grandmother.
She taught a young girl the names of all the wildflowers and
encouraged her to walk alone and unafraid through the woods.
She cherished books and poetry and had unfulfilled dreams
of being a writer someday . . . I hope she knows that
she helped to inspire me to become one instead.

∾

CONTENTS

Contents

The murmur of a bee,
A witchcraft yieldeth me . . .

EMILY DICKINSON

Acknowledgments

To my friends, who from the beginning encouraged me to write. To Rebecca and Cindy for their insights, listening to me babble and making me howl with laughter. To Colleen, my gardening buddy, who braved it out with me during our Master Gardener classes, and especially to Paula, who always demanded, "When are you going to write that book?" Thanks for all the support and faith in me. Also a high-tech thanks to Ben, our resident Computer Wizard, for all your assistance.

A special thanks goes to my magickal friends. For Amy, my fellow witch mom, and to her children. To Scott, with appreciation for the use of your library. To Mickie and her girls, and to Nicole, an incredibly talented garden witch. Thanks for your friendship, Nicole, and for your help with the bath salt recipes.

Also, I'd like to thank the ladies at Llewellyn: new submissions editor, Megan Atwood; my editor, Becky Zins; and Kerigwen, for the gorgeous artwork.

To my family, for your patience with me as I worked on this book. I'm grateful for your bearing with me while I shouted at the old computer and then made myself crazy trying to learn a new one. My loving appreciation goes to my two teenage sons, for always asking how the book was coming along, for the emergency computer lessons, and for unwavering encouragement and enthusiasm. To my magickal daughter Kat, whom I cherish. Thank you for pushing me to write the faerie chapter and for quietly pulling up a chair and offering to help make my spells rhyme.

Finally, to my husband, Ken. It's been a great twenty years. This is for making me laugh at the most inappropriate times of my life and for creating a wonderfully loud, boisterous, and happy family with me. I love you. Thanks for always believing . . . in both me and the magick.

Everything in nature invites us
constantly to be what we are.
GRETEL EHRLICH
~

Introduction

Picture for a moment the image of the benevolent witch who lives in a flower-surround-
ed cottage. The witch's gardens are a place where morning glories and moonflowers tumble
over privacy fences. Roses climb over handmade arbors, and magickal herbs and flowers
thrive together in sunny beds. Around back, tucked under old trees, the shade garden offers a
quiet spot and relief from the summer heat.

Ah . . . a suburban Pagan myth. I have read that this image of the witch
is outdated, over-romanticized, and unrealistic. Actually, it's very
real, and it's all true. I'm taking a stand. Honestly, my knees
are killing me. I am one of those witches who are supposedly a
suburban myth. I am a garden witch.

A garden witch? Is this some new, unheard-of tradition?
No. The lore of herbs and flowers is ancient, as is the practice
of growing a magickal garden. Gardens have always been
enchanting places. A garden witch just takes that theory and
runs with it. Magickal gardening is an intimate approach
to putting the nature back into your earth religion.

How do you know if you're a garden witch?
Well, the symptoms are fairly easy to diagnose. Do
you experience a sensory rush at the sights and smells

of a garden? Are you fascinated by plant lore and legend? Do you enjoy growing your own herbs and plants? To those of you who answered yes, and those of you future gardeners that yearn to try your hand at magickal gardening and herbalism, this will be right up your alley.

I'd like to invite you into the world of the garden witch—into my world. In this book you will find ideas, tips, and practical advice for both the magickal and the mundane gardener. There are garden witch spells and recipes, garden lore, seasonal crafts, and suggestions for simple sabbat celebrations that you can enjoy with your family.

Who am I to write on the subject of garden witchery? What are my qualifications? My name is Ellen Dugan. I live in Missouri with my husband and our three teenage children. I have many years of nursery and garden center experience, including contracting out occasionally as a landscape and garden designer. In the spring of 2000, I received Master Gardener status through the University of Missouri and my local county extension office.

I first began to seriously study folk magick in the late 1980s. I was initiated into Wicca standing under a full moon on Samhain/Halloween night. In the past, I have participated in an eclectic training group, and then organized and was a participant of a women's open circle. Currently I am a member of a wonderful circle of adult Wiccans and their families.

Years ago, when I had first begun practicing as a solitary witch, I stumbled across a book that forever changed the way I looked at gardening. It was Scott Cunningham's *Magical Herbalism*. In those early gardener days, I had just started to realize that most of my perennials were classified as herbs. Even more surprising to me was the fact that several of the magickal herbs listed in Cunningham's book were perennials and herbs that I already had growing in my yard. *Cool.*

With my newfound knowledge in hand, I made a list of all my annuals, perennials, and herbs. Hey, I'm a Virgo—we are really good at lists. Then I cross-referenced them to Cunningham's list, and what do you know? I had supplies!

All these great magickal ingredients, right at my fingertips. I was in garden witch heaven. And that is how it all began . . .

So, while your own gardening stories will be different, let's both stroll down this garden path together. I can't wait to show you how to add a little garden witchery into your life . . . from the ground up!

*Who bends a knee where violets grow
a hundred secret things shall know.*

RACHEL FIELD

What Is Garden Witchery?

For some folks, garden witchery conjures up images of lush, enchanted gardens where butterflies dance and children play. Wind chimes sing in the breeze and fountains trickle and splash. In this magickal place, the witch who lives there strolls about under sunny skies or dappled moonlight, gathering plants for her spellwork and for their fragrance. Fantasy? No. All of those things are possible in a city, suburban, or rural yard.

The gardens described for you in the introduction are real. I was describing my gardens. Suburban magickal gardens are a reality. You can do it. All it takes is hard work, determination, and time. Let's add two more very important magickal ingredients to this mixture: you and your imagination.

Use yours for a moment to visit me in my magickal gardens. Just come as you are. Let me assure you that I do not waft around the yard in ritual wear. Nor do I expect you to. How will you find me? I can usually be found working in the gardens, toting around a five-gallon bucket full of gardening supplies. I am typically crawling around on my hands and knees, attired in sturdy clothes and sunglasses. It's more than likely I'll either be planting, weeding, or dead-heading the gardens. I'm probably grubby and having a great time.

Sorry for the lack of mystique. There is no big drama here. I am a very down-to-earth type of witch. I have often been accused by my friends of being a cross between Martha Stewart and Samantha Stevens. You know, I can live with that.

Come on around back and sit with me under the shade of one of the old maples in the backyard. Let's plop down in the grass and chat. I suppose you have lots of questions . . . that great big chartreuse plant? That's a Sum and Substance hosta. Yeah, he is a monster. You like the silver gazing globe? Thanks, my kids gave it to me for Mother's Day last year. That fragrance? Ah . . . what does it smell like to you? Sort of an orange-floral? It could be the monarda, or is that scent you're noticing a captivating combination of soil, sunscreen, and bug spray? Why, that would be me.

So, you're here because you want to learn about magickal gardening? I have plenty to tell and to teach you. But first, I'd like you to look me in the eyes. Our eyes meet and hold. I smile and let out a contented sigh, and we both begin to laugh. Now let me see your hands, don't mind any garden soil that is still on mine . . .

I grasp your hands and turn over your palms to give them a steely eyed stare. No, I'm not looking for a green thumb. I'm looking to see if you have an open and loving heart, determination, and strong hands. That's what it takes to be a garden witch. The heart, I am sure, is just fine. As for the hands . . . trust me. If you are seriously determined to get into gardening, you will have those strong, capable hands soon enough.

A garden witch is not unlike a kitchen witch in that they both practice a hearth and home type of magick. However, don't let that fool you into complacency! A kitchen witch or garden witch on their home turf is an awesome magickal force indeed. Stay with me here, we are still talking about an advanced magickal system. Nothing winds me up faster than those who would sneer down at the home-based, family-oriented type of witches.

Practicing a down-to-earth, practical style of witchcraft is both enjoyable and fulfilling. There is nothing wrong with raising your family and quietly living the natural magician's life. How do you imagine the wisewomen of old lived? It's a pretty safe bet that they practiced alone and discreetly. (In the old days, it was safer that way.)

The solitary path is one that many modern witches find themselves walking today, some by choice, others by chance. It can be discouraging working by yourself without the benefit of a coven for support and advice. It can also be illuminating to go it alone. Use this time to expand your knowledge and understanding of the earth's magicks. Go ahead, get out there in the yard and plant some herbs. Stir up a little herbal magick in the kitchen, it's fun! You don't have to have an entourage along to expand your skills. You simply need yourself. Often the most important and powerful magick performed by a witch is done privately.

Some magickal folks hear the words "kitchen witch" and their brains just shut down. Oh, they might give you a patronizing smile and a pat on the head. Then they'll inform you how they've come a long way from their days of kitchen magick. Don't let them intimidate you.

Growing your own magickal plants and herbs and using them properly becomes a complex part of a major magickal working. It is true that working advanced magick requires more time, study, and effort on your part. That time and effort you put out to elevate your skills is well spent. It separates the novice from the adept practitioner.

Magickal herbalism in itself is considered to be a major magick. Major magicks are defined as those that require a higher level of knowledge and expertise. It may take months before your plants are ready to harvest. Magickal herbs have their own energies and correspondences to be considered as well. It requires discipline, patience, and competence to use plant energies effectively. Think about it.

So many witches are in a rush to learn a new spell or a new technique that they often overlook the obvious. It's not about the spells, it's about the magick. *Your* magick. Each person is drawn to a specialty in magick, or a favorite type of magick, if you will—something that just clicks for them. For some of us, it's herbs and gardening.

If you had to assemble herbs for a healing spell and you wanted a lot of magickal *oomph*, what do you think would be most likely to deliver it? Some dried lavender that you ordered online? Who knows what sort of chemicals could have been sprayed on the plants? Or how old the herb is? Or how many people handled it?

Instead, consider some homegrown lavender or yarrow that you would have tended yourself. We'll take this a step further and add that you harvested in a correct phase of the moon that corresponded with the results you were trying to achieve. Astrological timing plays a large part in garden witchery. These magickal herbs and flowers that you've grown can be further enhanced by the correct use of astrological timing. These will be discussed in detail in chapter 6.

There is nothing quite like making—or growing, for that matter—a magickal tool yourself. As you know, a self-created magickal tool or object becomes twice as powerful from absorbing the energy that you expended in the making of the item. So the same can be said for cultivating your own magickal flowers and herbs. As you sow, raise, and then harvest your herbs and plants, your energy has seeped into the plant every time you touched it. Now all that energy is waiting to be programmed or released.

Garden witches and natural magicians can be city dwellers working in community gardens as easily as suburban Pagans doing the "weekend warrior" thing in their backyards. The point is that you will be working in the garden, whether it's in pots and window boxes on your balcony, in the backyard, or on the farm. It doesn't matter where. It is the *quality* of the plants, not the quantity of them, that counts. Connecting with nature is our goal here. Sound good? Great! Roll up your sleeves and get ready to dig in.

Herbs and garden plants play a meaningful part in the folklore and tradition of every culture. Their arcane and phenomenal powers to heal the mind and body fascinate us and confirm humankind's connection to the natural world. A garden is a place that encourages and lures people to unearth the magick, mystery, and unexpected surprises that nature will reveal to anyone who wants to take a closer look. The garden does and will talk back, teaching us about success as well as failure. What do you imagine you could learn if we were to settle down in the grass, be still, and listen closely to Nature as she teaches us? You would discover many secret things and learn a myriad of valuable lessons. That's a good place to start, just don't stop there.

Now, how much more information, do you suppose, would be divined by getting out there and actually getting your hands dirty? As gardeners, be it magickal or mundane, we cultivate more than just herbs and flowers. We are cultivating a sensitivity and appreciation for the environment. By tapping into the magick of the earth, you increase your abilities and strengthen your magickal expertise. To "walk with power" means that you move in tune with the powers of nature, the powers of the Earth herself. This is a very important step toward becoming a responsible magician and a jubilant guardian of the Earth.

> *All the wild witches, those most noble ladies,*
> *For all their broomsticks and their tears,*
> *Their angry tears, are gone.*
>
> WILLIAM BUTLER YEATS

The Legacy of the Wisewomen

The history of herbalism begins at the dawn of time, when our earliest ancestors discovered that certain plants had a specific effect on their health and well-being. Other plants were found to comfort, had pleasant aromas, produced a colored dye, or were good to eat.

It is no surprise, then, that plants were thought to possess powers either for good or evil, and then became objects of reverence and worship. The trees especially, as they lived for much longer than a single human's life span. Most of the plants that were considered magickal were used for medicine rather than for foodstuff.

As magick and faith, biology and medicine, botany and philosophy all initially existed together rather than being thought of as separate sciences, rituals began around the harvesting and use of plants and herbs. To be the most effective they were picked at certain times of the year or prepared during specific cycles of the moon. The custodians of this knowledge were the first witches, the wisewomen.

The legacy of the wisewomen instills love and reverence for the Earth. From these lessons we learn the hidden meanings of the folk names of flowers and the legends of the trees, the uses of astrological timing, the portents of nature, and the creatures of the garden.

Traditionally, the witch was a solitary practitioner, a seer and the village wisewoman or cunning man. From their modest gardens they produced herbal amulets and charms for the common folk. Local practitioners birthed babies and cast their spells. They whispered herbal treatments to their clients and performed spells for love, healing, prosperity, and an abundant harvest.

How do we know what sort of Craft these wisewomen practiced? What varieties of plants did they actually grow? There really is no easy answer, but I have a good idea where to look for clues. We must try to find the truth between the much-maligned historical figure of the witch and her modern counterpart of today.

Gothic Plants and Their Magickal Alternatives

Historically, witch plants carry a sinister reputation, such as belladonna, foxglove, and deadly nightshade. Hemlock, monkshood, and the yew with its berries are all beautiful plants and all extremely toxic. Unfortunately, witches were often accused of being poisoners. Yikes!

I have read gardening and herb books that only list those types of plants as "witch" plants. How very narrow-minded and unfair of them.

Well, you're thinking, *who would grow such plants today?* If you walk into your local nursery with a list of plants like that, they are going to get real suspicious. Once I had someone do that to me. After I stopped gaping, I wrote down a reading list for her and then we had a nice little chat (my kids would tell you that means a lecture) about magickal plant alternatives to gothic witch garden plants.

Yes, many common plants and shrubs are poisonous. Some you may not even know or suspect, like azaleas, morning glories, and lily of the valley. If you have children or pets, I urge you to be cautious with your plantings. Do your homework.

I contacted the Missouri Botanical Garden for a list of poisonous plants. They sent me their list and a list from the Missouri Poison System. Call the Master Gardeners in your area for advice. Master Gardeners usually are based out of a University Extension Office. These offices operate individually out of their own specific counties. Check the phone book for a "University Outreach" or "Local Extension Office." Ask if they can mail you some information. Also, in chapter 5, there is a quick index of poisonous garden plants for you to refer to.

Tradition and Craft history are fine, but you want to use a big dose of common sense as well. Sure, we all want an ambience of tradition, and want to know what those old witch gardens were really like. What sort of plants did they contain? Remember those alternatives I mentioned? Believe it or not, we get our answers from those clues at an unlikely source: medieval gardens.

I know a bank where the wild thyme blows,
Where oxlips and the nodding violet grows,
Quite over-canopied and luscious woodbine,
With sweet musk-roses and eglantine.

SHAKESPEARE,
A MIDSUMMER NIGHT'S DREAM

~

Ye Olde Medieval Gardens

Medieval gardens weren't that different from our magickal or mundane gardens of today. Remember that these were *working* gardens. They fed the family. Fruit trees provided the cherry, pear, plum, and apple, favorite medieval fruits. Vegetables such as beets, radishes, beans, cabbage, and carrots were cultivated.

Herbs such as angelica and lavender were planted for medicinal, aromatic, and seasoning values. Angelica is an archaic and highly aromatic herb that was believed to possess angelic powers and was once worn as an amulet for protection against evil spells. It has the astrological correspondence of the sun. Angelica stems and seeds were used as flavorings, and the stalks were candied and eaten. This plant was also utilized for its aromatic properties derived from its flowers and leaves, both for perfume and potpourri. Magickally, you may draw upon the natural energy of angelica's blooms and leaves for healing and protection spells.

Lavender was cultivated not only for scent but for medicine. Its oil is a strong antiseptic with antibacterial properties. It was used to treat all manner of cuts, scrapes, infections, and colds. The scent of lavender has traditionally been employed to help ease headaches and to mask unpleasant odors. Lavender was and still is a popular flower for potpourri and cosmetics. Lavender has the planetary correspondence of Mercury, and it may be worked into any enchantments designed for love, happiness, and peace.

The rose is a symbol of love and of secrets. Traditionally, a white rose has the ruling planet of the moon. A red rose belongs to Jupiter, and a damask rose relates to Venus. In olden times, rose petals were used to treat a plethora of ailments. The petals were added to salads, crystallized, and made into syrup, preserves, and vinegars. The petals were also added to soaps and cosmetics. Rose water was added for flavoring in sauces and sweet dishes. The oil was applied to chapped skin and, of course, for perfumes.

Other common varieties of medieval herbs were mullein, fennel, yarrow, mint, tansy, rosemary, parsley, sage, dill, and thyme, all of which, I am happy to point out, are today used as magickal herbs. Some types of medieval flowers that were (and still are) popular include the iris, lily, poppy, peony, columbine, delphinium, and the violet.

You know the violet, that great little flower that pops up in your lawn and flower beds in the spring? Unfortunately considered a weed today, the violet has the following magickal properties: love, happiness, and faery magick. The sweet violet is a herald of spring and a Venus plant. It has been cultivated for its perfume and color, and is added to cosmetics, drinks, and syrups. To the ancient Greeks, it was a symbol of fertility. Among the more popular perfume scents used in Victorian England, the violet was venerated by the old herbalists, who all spoke with great affection for this beguiling little purplish-blue flower.

Today, you may gather violet blooms, wash them gently, and toss them into salads. Or pat them dry, dip them into fine sugar, and freeze them. They may be used to decorate cakes, or you may put the fresh blooms inside of ice cube trays. Fill them up with water and freeze for a fun way to accent cold drinks at a garden party. Violets are often a child's favorite flower and are worth saving a small section of your garden for.

Take another look at that listing of medieval herbs. Many types of medieval herbs are readily available today as improved modern varieties. So where do you find them? Try checking out a nursery or garden center. It *is* just that easy. Magickal plants are everywhere.

Garden Witch Magicks

Today, garden witch magicks include working with natural objects such as trees, flowers, plants, stones, and crystals. The garden witch or natural magician lives their lives by celebrating the magick of nature, attuning to the rhythms of the changing seasons, growing their plants and herbs, and giving out magickal advice for specific needs. The garden witch's magickal gifts are handmade and homegrown.

What sort of garden witch skills will you be learning? Why, I thought you'd never ask. Of course we'll include practical tips for magickal gardening and suggestions for magickal plants. You'll find several lists for enchanted herbs, trees, and flowers that are easy to grow and that you can achieve new-gardener success with, as well as ideas for magickal plants that will thrive in sunny gardens and recommendations for mysterious, bewitching shade gardens.

We'll discuss faery magick—I want to share some advice and some anecdotes. We'll cover astrological timing, a kicked-up variety of color magick, and the language of flowers, including a whole chapter on flower magick. There will be theme gardens for you to sample, such as faery, tussie-mussie, and children's Samhain gardens.

We'll want to refresh your understanding of aromatherapy, so you'll find little gems of aromatherapy information sprinkled throughout this book. I want to give you some ideas for witchy-type garden crafts and tools that you can easily make and use, along with houseplant magick and fresh flower spells . . . as a matter of fact, let's get you started right now.

The Magick of House Plants and Fresh Flowers

House plants and fresh flowers perform wonderful magick. Add a little of that old garden witch magick power and ta-da! A potently enchanted present!

Among the common house plants that have magickal correlations are the African violet, for spirituality and protection. The spider plant absorbs negativity. Ferns are protective. Ivy is for fidelity and fertility. The aloe plant is lucky and wards off accidents in the home. A ficus tree has many magickal correspondences, including love and good luck, and it guards against your family ever going hungry. (Unless, of course, you have teenagers.)

Perhaps you know of a couple who is trying to conceive. The gift of a blooming cyclamen along with instructions to keep the plant in the bedroom would be very appropriate. Cyclamen promotes fertility, happiness, and lust—perfect for the hopeful parents-to-be.

Is a friend suffering through a breakup? A small clay pot that you've planted full of sunny-faced pansies will brighten things up. Pansies are sacred to Cupid and have the folk name of heartsease—they are a sure cure for those that ache through the disappointment of a romance gone sour. You could paint magickal symbols on the container if you like, pentacles and yellow crescent moons. Try adding symbols for friendship and healing or, better yet, ones of your own design.

We all know what the red rose symbolizes: lust, love, and romance. Did you know the magickal correspondences change with the many different colors of the rose? This inventory is adapted from the traditional language of flowers for my own garden witchery. Study this list and see what else you can add to it.

WHITE: Peace, love, and new beginnings

YELLOW: Joy and happiness

ORANGE: Vitality and energy

PINK: Innocent love and friendship

PURPLE: Power and passion

IVORY: Romance and steadfast, mature love

The garden witch utilizes her* knowledge of color magick and magickal aromatherapy in designing spells of her own creation. For instance, giving a few red carnations to a friend who is ill is not only thoughtful, it's downright magickal. Why? Red is a healing color and the scent of carnations is an energy booster. Fresh carnations come in a wide variety of colors, are easy to obtain and, most importantly, are an inexpensive magickal flower.

It's up to you to decide whether to give the plant or flowers as is and let the natural scent and energy of them do their work, or whether you choose to magickally enhance them. Please remember to make sure the person receiving such an enchanted plant is open to the idea. If you give purposely zapped flowers or plants to a nonmagickal friend or person that is unknowing and unaware, that's manipulation, folks.

When looking for fresh ingredients for garden witchery, hit your own backyard first. See what you can find. Be creative. The wisewomen of old, sometimes referred to as hedge witches, utilized the components that were available to them: their gardens and the native plants and trees in the forests around them.

Unlike us, they didn't have access to the wide variety of plants and flowers that we often take for granted. If you don't have a certain plant, perennial, or tree, and it's one that you'd like to own, you may find yourself taking a trip to the local nursery or garden center.

For fresh flowers out of season, try the florist. Use whatever is available to you and within your budget. You don't have to spend a lot of money to practice garden witchery.

The path of the garden witch is a valid one. There is no reason why a sincere, modern practitioner should shy away from it. When all is said and done, a garden witch must be confident in her own abilities and possess a strong link to the earth and divinity. If you want to flex your magickal muscles and learn advanced magickal skills, this could be just what the witch doctor ordered.

---

* When I say "her," it's because I'm writing this book from my perspective—no disrespect intended for the guys. Many of the best gardeners that I know are male, like my husband and father-in-law (you should see their vegetable gardens)!

2

The only limit to your garden
is the boundaries of your imagination.
THOMAS D. CHURCH
☙

backyard magick

There are many magickal perennials, annuals, and herbs—even trees and shrubs—that are easy to grow. Where do you find them? You may not have to look very far at all; maybe not any farther than your own backyard. Magickal plants aren't all exotic little numbers that are impossible to find. They are readily available and all around you.

Starting a magickal garden isn't difficult either. A magickal garden may be any size or style that you like—formal or cottage style. Formal flower beds have distinct geometric planting patterns, such as circles, squares, a hexagon or triangle. (Picture a Victorian knot garden or a formal rose garden.) Long, straight lines and borders of hedges, such as boxwood, are often worked into the design or layout.

Informal flower beds are characterized by curved and free-flowing lines, free-formed flower bed edges, and more casual and relaxed color combinations and varying plant heights all mixed in together. A good example would be an English cottage garden. I must confess I prefer cottage style. It's romantic and casual with all those flowers growing close together.

Cottage favorites include old-fashioned varieties that your grandmother would have grown in her yard, like hollyhocks, lilac bushes, climbing roses, and tiger lilies, just to name a few. Do you think she knew that they are all magickal plants? You might find it interesting to note that in the language of flowers, the hollyhock stands for ambition. The lilac signifies first love. Climbing roses symbolize the tenacity of love, and tiger lilies are for erotic love. Wow.

Adding accessories to an existing garden like wind chimes, a bench, an affordable café table and chair set, or even a small fountain will go a long way toward removing your backyard from the mundane world into a magickal sanctuary. Privacy fences or tall shrubs and trees will give the garden seclusion and a sense of retreat for magickal workings . . . your very own magickal garden, can you imagine it?

The image that comes to my mind is of the witch raising her arms in supplication to a full moon that sails overhead. A fragrant breeze scented with roses stirs the wind chimes in her garden and gently blows her hair back from her serene, tranquil face.

As she begins her ritual, the incense smoke billows upward and the candles flicker softly. The crickets are singing and all of nature becomes calm and reverently quiet, as if sensing the witch's total, unshakable concentration . . .

"Hey, Mom!"

I just lost my fantasy image. I pull myself out of the scene I'm trying to create to be confronted by one of my teenage sons.

"Mom!" He repeats as I try to focus on him. "I need new football shoes," he informs me.

I frantically hit *save* on the computer and wonder what time it is. *They're home already? Where did my day off go?* "What?" I ask.

My daughter comes bounding in behind her brother, chattering nonstop about her day. "Oh, good," she says. "You're not working." And now that she's spotted me, I'm doomed.

I have a split second to reply and—damn, it's gone.

She takes a breath and launches into a full-scale, fast-paced account of her day. Her backpack hits the table with a thud. I try to catch up.

"Sorry, you need *how* many new folders?" I ask.

"Mom." With the long-suffering sigh that only a thirteen-year-old can produce, she rattles off her list again.

"Mom, my shoes?" My son tries to wedge his way back into the conversation. My daughter yells at him not to interrupt. His response is short, rude, and . . . wow, creative.

"That's enough," I start to say, only to be ignored. Oh, good. Now they've turned on each other.

Ah, domestic bliss. The plight of the modern witch, surrounded by the demands of family, spouse, and job. You try to grab time for yourself and your magick whenever and however you can. Sometimes you have to wait for those little darlings to go to bed so you can find some peace and quiet. It is not a lifestyle for the timid. No, sir. You really want to throw some danger into your life? Add three teenagers.

We don't always have the time or the funds to run to the store for our occult supplies. Wouldn't it be great if those supplies were right in your own backyard? They could be. Start thinking in terms of backyard magick.

> *The main purpose of a garden is to*
> *give its owner the best and highest kind*
> *of earthly pleasure.*
> GERTRUDE JEKYLL

Meet Your Magickal Yard

As a working mother, wife, and witch, I often look to the simplest of nature's supplies to fill my magickal needs. My garden is usually the first place I go. Take a walk around the yard and see what treasures you find. Changing leaves, crunchy pine cones, maybe a fallen feather, a perfect rosebud. How can you incorporate these things into magick? Use your imagination.

All those herbs, flowers, and trees are waiting for you to notice them. There is more to the trees in your yard than sheltering the home and increasing the property value. Trees are magick. The structure or bones of a garden are its trees. They provide habitat, food, and shelter for wildlife, as well as supplies for the garden witch.

Trees are among a witch's very best friends. Tree magick is accessible and user friendly. No excuses, now, just about everybody has access to a tree or two. If not in the backyard, dare I mention the park?

Nature is sacred. This is one of those lessons you should remember from your neophyte witch days. I have the hardest time trying to get folks to understand. Get off of your computers for a few hours. Reconnect with the Earth. Do one simple thing that will change the way you view your earth religion . . . guess what that is? Go outside! Nature is waiting for you. The God and Goddess are all around you.

The blue jays and cardinals raiding the bird feeder have a message for you. The butterflies that take refuge in your flower garden are happy to see you. Feel the breeze; refreshing, isn't it? Listen. What do you hear? Was that the neighbor's cat just romping in the catnip? Uh-oh, now my two cats are glaring at me to let them go play in the garden. Breathe deep, what do you smell? The neighbors' barbecue? Chimney smoke? Roses? Do you see the new crescent in the western sky tonight at sunset? Isn't she lovely? Get those five-plus senses involved. If you want to work in harmony with nature, you need to become aware of the natural world around you.

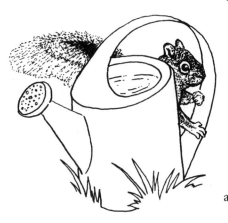

An excellent exercise for a new witch or one who needs a jumpstart to get them tuned back in to nature is to go outside and observe the night sky for ten minutes every night for a month. If you want to start at the new moon and go to the next new moon, that's good also.

Garden Witchery Quiz

Let's consider this a little homework assignment for you. You can get your hands dirty and start thinking garden witch thoughts. Here are some questions for you to look up and answer. Go crazy—buy yourself a spiral notebook for seventy-nine cents and write down your answers or use the space provided in the gardening journal beginning on page 205. Also, you could use this book for note keeping on your moon gazing for a month.

1. What direction does your house/apartment face?

2. Where does the sun rise and set at your house (front, side, or back)?

3. What phase is the moon in right now? (It doesn't count if you looked this question up and then wrote down the answer. You should know this one cold!)

4. Do you have trees in your yard? How many? What kind?

5. What species of birds show up at the bird feeder? What is your state bird?

6. Do you have any perennials in your yard or flowers growing in pots or baskets? What are they? What variety of grass (as in your lawn) do you have in your yard?

7. What is the soil like? Do you have loam or clay? Is it sandy or rocky?

8. (Bonus question) What cold hardiness zone do you live in?

Answers . . . and More Questions

The point of the previous questions was to get you thinking. I bet you knew a lot of the answers. If not—well, you wanted to learn something new, didn't you? The reason for questions number one and two is to have you pay attention to where your sun and shade patterns fall on your property, to ensure that you plant the right flower, herb, or shrub in the correct spot. For instance, if you wanted to plant a hydrangea shrub, where do you suppose would be the best location for planting? Hydrangeas thrive in afternoon shade. Do you even know where you have full afternoon shade? Better head outside and check it out.

Get a piece of paper and draw out a rough map of your home, or use this book's journal. You are going to make a map of your shade patterns. Relax, this doesn't have to be fancy. Begin at 8:00 A.M. and draw in any shaded areas that you may have. Check your yard every two hours and adjust the shady areas with dashed lines as the day progresses. (Note the time as you go along.) Keep track of the sun and shade patterns until 6:00 P.M. that evening. There, now you have a better idea of where you can successfully plant those shade- and sun-loving plants.

Grab a shovel and turn over a small section of your future garden. What's out there? Are you going to have to amend the soil? You'll want to get some organic matter back into the soil to encourage healthy plant growth, improve drainage, and make your soil easier to work with.

What should you look for? Every yard is unique with its soil requirements. I suggest going to a reputable nursery and asking what they recommend for your area. It's a pretty safe bet that composted manure, humus, and some topsoil will be on that list. These inexpensive soil amendments are found in most garden centers across the country. If you need a large quantity of topsoil you may want to consider buying it in bulk. Or check a local nursery and find out how much they charge to have topsoil delivered.

Remember to work these amendments into the soil that you already have. Turn over the soil, break up the large pieces, and work the amendments *down into* your existing soil. If you have a large bed planned or are worried that it may be too much for you to handle by your-self, call in a few friends. Try using a rototiller. They make short work of this type of situation. Rent one if necessary. Or add those amendments to your soil the old-fashioned way: with a shovel, a hoe, and a rake.

The last question on your quiz addresses the cold hardiness zone. You have seen these maps before. Every gardening magazine has one. A cold hardiness zone map is a map of the United States that shows the average minimum winter temperatures.

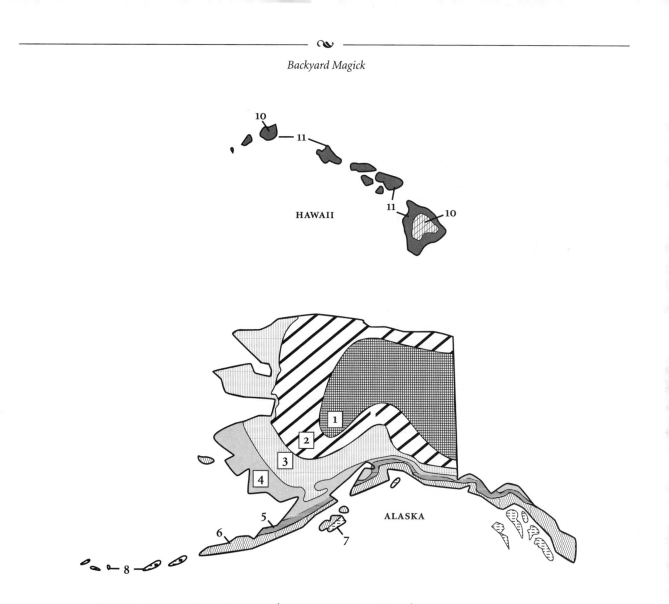

ALASKA AND HAWAII ZONE MAP (SEE PAGE 21 FOR CODES)

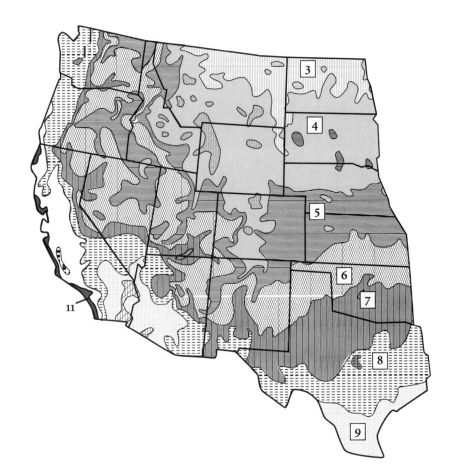

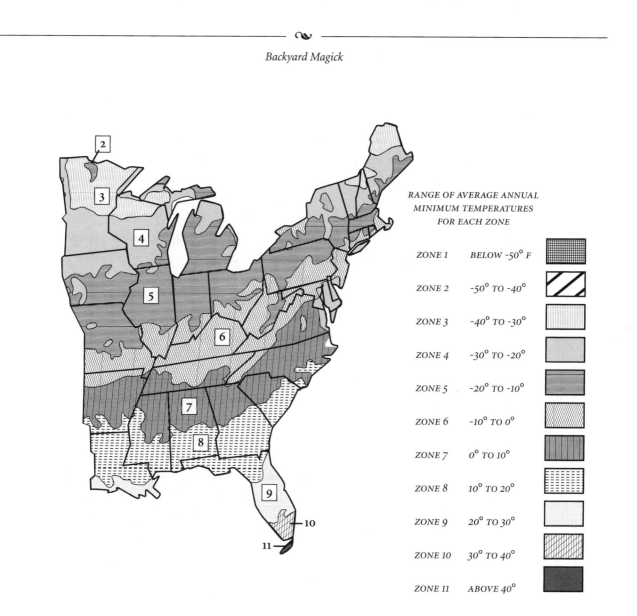

RANGE OF AVERAGE ANNUAL
MINIMUM TEMPERATURES
FOR EACH ZONE

ZONE 1   BELOW -50° F

ZONE 2   -50° TO -40°

ZONE 3   -40° TO -30°

ZONE 4   -30° TO -20°

ZONE 5   -20° TO -10°

ZONE 6   -10° TO 0°

ZONE 7   0° TO 10°

ZONE 8   10° TO 20°

ZONE 9   20° TO 30°

ZONE 10   30° TO 40°

ZONE 11   ABOVE 40°

Plants can be classified as either hardy or nonhardy, depending on their ability to withstand cold temperatures. Before you purchase a new plant, check the plant tags for zone requirements. If the plant tag lists a higher number than the zone that you live in, the plant will probably not survive your winter season. For example, if you live in zone 5 and you pick up a shrub that says it is only hardy to zone 7, then you have a great likelihood of losing that plant to winter injury. Winter injury can occur to nonhardy plants if winter temperatures are too low or if unseasonably low temperatures occur in fall or late spring.

Being aware of the shade patterns, your soil type, and what cold hardiness zone you live in are important tools to help you achieve success in the garden. Go on, do your homework and let's get ready to garden.

> *He that plants trees*
> *loves others besides himself.*
> THOMAS FULLER
>
> ∽

Trees

Question number four of our garden witchery quiz asked about trees. What species of trees do you have at home—old maples and elms? Do you have any blooming trees, like a pink flowering crab? You don't have just one tree, standing out in the middle of your yard like a lone soldier, do you? Maybe we should get him some company. If you don't have any trees in your yard or you'd like to add a few to the landscape, go to a nursery and pick some out. How about a magickal tree? Or would you prefer an ornamental? I promise you, anybody can plant a tree. I'll tell you how.

Clip the wire cage off of the root ball. Next, dig the hole as deep as the root ball and twice as wide. Ease in the tree, then straighten or turn as needed. Amend your soil with some composted manure mixed into the dirt that you took out of the hole. Root stimulator is good also; follow the directions on the package for amounts. Fill in with soil around the tree, pat the soil around the ball down firmly, and water in well.

Don't forget to keep watering. The nursery can instruct you as to the proper amount. But remember, a sprinkler for the lawn is not the way to water a tree. (Your grass will soak up all that water, the tree won't get any of it.) Use a bucket, pour it in slowly. Primitive, yes, but much more effective. Most dead tree returns to nurseries happen because the homeowner didn't water the tree correctly, or at all.

Here is a short index of trees and their magickal properties. Check your quiz answers and jot down the magickal associations of the trees that you have at home. In this list I tried to specify trees that are usually easy to find and common to most of the United States. For a more complete listing, I recommend Scott Cunningham's *Encyclopedia of Magical Herbs*. It's quite simply the best.

> *I think that I shall never see*
> *a poem lovely as a tree.*
>
> JOYCE KILMER
>
> ∾

Common Magickal Trees

APPLE (*Pyrus*). The apple tree is a favorite witch tree. There are many different species and cultivars of the apple. For the average homeowner, growing a dwarf fruit tree is often the most practical, as they bear full-sized fruit and take up less space in the yard. A good apple to try is Golden Delicious. This tree is described as self-fruiting and is often used as a pollinator tree for other apple varieties. The Golden Delicious apple performs well in the cold hardiness zones of 5 to 9. Also a great wood for a magickal wand, the associations of the apple tree are love, health, and garden magick.

Traditionally, a secret way to let someone know that you are a witch is to cut an apple crosswise. The seeds inside are arranged in the shape of a star. The fruit is employed at Mabon and Samhain, and in love spells (see page 63 for a Halloween love spell). A favorite family tradition at my house is to take the family apple picking on the first day of fall, the sabbat of Mabon.

BAY (*Laurus nobilis*). Also known as sweet bay and bay laurel. In the cold hardiness zones of 8–10 in the United States, this evergreen tree can grow from six to twenty-five feet tall, if protected from winter winds. Smaller, container-size plants are adaptable to being grown in pots and make for lovely topiaries. Grow bay outside in the summer and bring indoors as a houseplant in the winter. The bay tree or the woody potted shrub has dense bright green, rather leathery leaves. The bay tree was sacred to the God Apollo. It has the associations of prophecy, poetry, and healing. A wreath of bay leaves became the symbol of excellence for athletes and poets.

BIRCH (*Betula pendula*). The silver birch is a charming and graceful tree with its silvery-white bark and oval-shaped leaves. It may grow twenty to sixty feet in height and the leaves are a lovely shade of yellow in the fall. A traditional broom wood for witches, the wood is also used for Yule logs as well as maypoles. This is also a Goddess tree. The birch is an excellent tree for protection and purification. Zones 2–7.

DOGWOOD (*Cornus florida*). The dogwood grows up to thirty feet in height and is a very popular tree in the nursery trade. Spectacular off-white flowers will appear before the leaves unfold. Shiny, medium-sized fruits will show up in the fall, and the birds will thank you for them. The fall foliage is a luminous scarlet. There are pink varieties of the dogwood as well, though the white ones are tougher.

The dogwood tree prefers *shade*. They require the dappled shade from other taller trees or at least full afternoon shade. (I don't care what the guy at the nursery says!) The number one dead tree return at *every* nursery that I have ever worked for is the pink flowering dogwood. The reason? The trees were planted in full all-day sun, and the customers didn't water them properly. If you want a pink, blooming tree for full sun, try a crab apple instead. (The magickal associations for the crab apple would be the same as the apple. See above.)

The magickal properties of the dogwood are love and protection. Cultivate this blooming tree in your garden to promote a loving and happy home environment. In the language of flowers, the dogwood signifies durability. The dogwood thrives in zones 5–9.

ELDER (*Sambucus nigra*). This small tree grows to fifteen feet. It bears clusters of star-shaped, off-white flowers in early summer, which are followed by dark purple berries in the fall. The berries are high in vitamin C and are utilized in cooking. Elderberries are a popular fruit for jellies and wine making, and it's a common wild plant that is included in many different country's magickal plant folklores. Sacred to the Mother and Crone Goddesses, the elder tree has the magickal properties of love and blessings. The leaves and berries are used for protection and in breaking spells that were cast against you. Growing an elder in the garden will protect your property from misfortune and harm. Zones 3–8.

ELM (*Ulmus campestris*). A tree reported to be popular with the elves, its folk name is elven. Used primarily for love and dream work, this tree is not as popular as it once was, due to Dutch elm disease, which almost wiped out the species in the 1950s. The elm is supposed to protect you from lightning; however, I recommend that you keep them pruned (that's *pruned*, not topped—see Topping Trees, page 29) to avoid damage from breaking limbs during high winds. Zones 3–10.

HAWTHORN (*Crataegus* spp.). Valued for their lavish flowers, fruits, and attractive growth habits, hawthorns are dense and thorny. They can be difficult to find in most modern-day nurseries, due to the huge thorns that cover the upper trunk and the branches. If you don't have any luck locating one, try the Conservation Department instead. If you have an adult hawthorn in your yard, clip off the low-growing thorns to keep your children safe. Zones 4–7. (This zone information may vary slightly for the many different species of the hawthorn.)

The hawthorn tree has a long magickal history. The trinity of faery trees are the oak, the ash, and the thorn. It is said that where these three trees grow together, you would gain the power to see the faeries. Happiness and fertility are the magical associations of this tree.

MAPLE (*Acer*). There are several varieties of the maple, including the following: the common silver maple (*Acer saccharinum*), a wonderful shade tree and a staple in many a yard of older homes like mine. The leaves transform into a soft yellow in the fall. With the sugar maple (*Acer saccharum*), the sap of this tree may be boiled down to make maple syrup and sugar. The sugar maple's changing leaves may turn anywhere from a bright yellow to a fire-red color during the fall months. Lastly, there is the red maple (*Acer rubrum*), one of the first trees to change into a brilliant red color in Missouri. Maple leaves of all varieties are used in love spells and for prosperity work. The branches are often used to create magickal wands. Magickally used to sweeten things up. Zones 4–8.

OAK (*Quercus* spp.). The oak is considered the king of trees, and may grow up to 110 feet tall. There are many varieties of oak trees, such as English oak, pin oak, red oak, scarlet oak, and the white oak. Check and see which of these varieties are best suited to your climate. Zones 3 or 4–9. (The zones will vary according to the variety of the oak.)

Sacred to the Druids and the God, oak wood can be made into a powerful wand, or a small twig may be carried to bring about good fortune. Acorns are charms for fertility, sexual potency, protection from storms, and are amulets for youthfulness and beauty.

PINE (*Pinus* spp.). The pine may be easily discerned from other evergreens because their needlelike leaves are produced in bundles of two to five needles. They require full sun to grow and look their best. The tree of protection and money, many prosperity spells call for pine. Isn't that handy? A lot of green candles are pine scented. Pine needles may be burned to cleanse your home of unwanted astral nasties or bad vibrations. Pines may be used in the garden or yard as specimen trees, as a screen, or for a wind break. Also, most types of evergreens make excellent habitats for birds and other local wildlife. Cold hardiness zone requirements will differ from species to species. On average, zones 3–7.

ROWAN, OR EUROPEAN MOUNTAIN ASH (*Sorbus aucuparia*). This tree is worth growing in your yard, as it has four-season interest: flowers in the spring, green leaves in the summer, and reddish foliage in the fall. It bears small orange-red berries that are prized by birds throughout the late fall and winter months. Zones 3–7.

Traditionally the rowan is thought to be a witch tree. It is a tree of the Goddess and is sacred to the faeries. A rowan growing near a stone circle is considered to be the most powerful. The rowan protects from all sources of evil. Two rowan twigs tied into an equal-armed cross with red thread is a powerful protective amulet. The berries are used in charm bags for power, healing, and protection.

WILLOW (*Salix alba*). The willow enjoys growing near the water and has the planetary association of the moon. Therefore, wands made out of willow branches are for moon magick. The willow is sacred to many moon goddesses, including Artemis, Lilith, and Hecate. The leaves are a charm for love. All parts of this tree—twigs, leaves, and branches—may be used as amulets for protection from evil. Zones 2–9.

WITCH HAZEL (*Hamamelis virginiana*). A fragrant, late-winter bloomer, these hardy trees may grow thirty feet tall by twenty-five feet across. This tree starts out with ribbonlike yellow blooms in late February–early March. It then has oval-shaped leaves all summer and ends the season with luminous yellow foliage in the fall. The witch hazel will thrive in sun to part shade. It is an intriguing addition to an informal garden or a smashing addition to a woodland garden. This species is hardy in zones 3–8.

According to folklore and legend, the witch hazel is a tree of learning, poetry, fire, loveliness, and fertility. Traditionally this tree is associated with benevolent witchcraft. Its wood is often used for divining rods.

To the Druids, trees were sacred—especially the oak and the mistletoe that grow there. The Druids divided their year into thirteen lunar months, each month having its own tree. There were the seven noble trees of Ireland and, last but not least, we have the nine sacred woods for a magickal fire.

In this anonymous poem, we find more hints as to the magickal folklore of nine various trees, or woods. Read the poem carefully: the woods and their properties are listed. Consider the associations as you choose wood for a new wand or lay your next magickal fire into the fireplace.

THE POEM OF THE NINE WOODS

Nine woods in the cauldron go, burn them fast and burn them slow.

Birch into the fire goes, to represent what the Lady knows.

Oak gives the forest might, in the fire brings the God's insight.

Rowan is the tree of power, causing life and magic to flower.

Willows at the waterside stand, to aid the journey to the Summerland.

Hawthorn is burned to purify, and draw faery to your eye.

Hazel, the tree of wisdom and learning, adds its strength to the bright fire burning.

White are the flowers of the apple tree, that brings us the fruits of fertility.

Grapes that grow upon the vine, giving us both joy and wine.

Fir does mark the evergreen, to represent immortality unseen.

Elder is the Lady's tree, burn it not, or cursed you'll be.

Topping Trees
(Boo! Hiss!)

Topping—or "heading," "tipping," and "rounding over"—is perhaps the most harmful tree pruning practice known. Topping is the indiscriminate cutting back of tree branches to stubs. In truth, topping does the following to trees:

IT STRESSES TREES. Removing 50–100 percent of the leaf-bearing crown of a tree *starves* the tree. Leaves produce "food" for the tree, so no leaves equals no food. If the tree does not have enough stored energy reserves, topping the tree will weaken it and the tree may die. Also, stressed trees are more vulnerable to insects and disease.

TOPPING CAUSES DECAY. Few trees can defend the multiple wounds caused by topping. This leaves the tree open to decay, which encourages those insects and diseases mentioned before.

TOPPING CREATES HAZARDS. The new shoots will grow quickly and they are very prone to breakage.

TOPPING IS JUST PLAIN UGLY! Topping removes the ends of the branches and leaves ugly stubs. Topping destroys the natural shape of the tree; the tree will never regain its natural form.

Enchanting Backyard Plants

Wait, we're not finished yet. What about shrubs and ground cover? No, I'm not kidding. Other garden plants have great magickal potential as well.

The *AZALEA* and *RHODODENDRON* are evergreens (zones 5–8). They hold much of their foliage all winter. A staple in many southern gardens, they remind me of hospitality and gracious homes. For something different, try floating the blooms in bowls of water to attract garden spirits and faeries.

FORSYTHIAS are harbingers of spring. Those yellow blooms are so welcome after winter's dreariness. Use them for any spells that are for new projects, new beginnings, or for making a fresh start. You can force the stems to bloom a couple of weeks early if you cut a few stems and bring them inside to your warm house. In a few days they will bloom out. Remember to change the water often. Forsythias thrive in zones 3–8.

The *HOLLY* can be a shrub or grown as a standard tree, depending on the variety. The holly is used in Yule decorations, wreaths, swags, and to decorate the Yule log. To grow a holly in your garden is to bring good luck. It is also a protective herb. Rumor has it that holly leaves were once called "bat wings," so if you ever run into any old spells that call for bat's wings, you'll know what they really mean. Zones 5 or 6–9.

HYDRANGEAS come in several varieties. Big Leaf hydrangea is the species that is familiar to most gardeners. The blooms may be pink or blue, depending on your soil acidity content. If you want blue flowers, try the Nikko Blue variety and add soil acidifier like Mir-acid to the soil. The magickal association of this plant is hex-breaking. Use the dried bark from the dormant stems in the winter for this purpose. Zones 5–9.

LILACS are utilized for protection and to keep ghosts at bay, and they are a faery favorite. The scent of lilacs is used to promote clairvoyance. A traditional cottage garden plant, they come in many colors and sizes. A new variety is available called Tinkerbell; it is pinkish-purple and very fragrant. Zones 3–8.

The VIBURNUM is also for protection and has a colorful magickal history as well. In England they were planted close to barn doors to protect the cattle from being bewitched. Viburnums are great shady garden shrubs. A fragrant type called Korean Spice will make small clusters of pinkish-white blooms in the spring, green textured foliage in the summer, and red leaves plus berries for the birds in the fall. Zones 4–8.

> *Heaven is under our feet*
> *as well as over our heads.*
> HENRY DAVID THOREAU

Ground Covers

Ground covers are often overlooked when people talk about magickal plants.

PERIWINKLE is a very popular ground cover that is also an extremely powerful magickal herb. It goes by the botanical name of *Vinca minor*. This ground cover blooms heavily in the spring and again lightly in the fall. Another name for this is the sorcerer's violet. The blooms of this shade-loving ground cover are purple with little white stars inside. Utilized in all kinds of magick, the periwinkle can be applied in bindings, protection work, love spells, and prosperity. Zones 4–8.

AJUGA. An herbal ground cover, *Ajuga reptans* is another easy-to-find plant. It is sometimes called bugle weed. This purple flowering plant is very attractive to bees. Long ago the crushed flowers were made into a salve for bruises. I would caution against consuming this herb, as it is thought to be mildly narcotic. Bugleweed comes in pink flowering varieties as well. Magickally use this for healing and health spells. Zones 4–10.

SWEET WOODRUFF (*Galium odorata*) is a hardy perennial and a great plant for semi-shady gardens. A popular ground cover, woodruff has a dusky vanilla scent when it blooms and is considered a protective charm for athletes. Woodruff attracts wealth and victory. This attractive woodland plant was used for its scent in olden times. It was strewn on floors, hung in churches, added to potpourri, and stuffed into bedding. Zones 4–8.

Gathering Guidelines—Harm None

Now that I've given you this information, we should touch on a few gathering guidelines. If you do not have access to trees or shrubs in your own yard, do not look at this as a license to go and raid whatever tree you find outside of your yard. A leaf or two is one thing, but if you get caught snipping blooms off shrubs or cutting or breaking small limbs and branches off trees in your local park, you will probably face a fine.

If you don't know how to correctly prune a branch from a tree or a shrub, I recommend that you learn. Go read up on it or have someone show you how. If you purposely damage a tree while taking supplies for magickal workings, I sincerely doubt that your magick is going to work. Remember that "harm none" applies to all living things, and plants and trees are definitely living.

If you are gathering on private property, always get permission from the owner. Otherwise it's stealing! Bring a tree identification guide with you. These are inexpensive and a must-have. Use a sharp, clean knife or garden scissors. Take only the smallest amount of plant material that you will need. Also, do not cut or dig up wildflowers, as some of our native species are protected by law.

Make sure that you have plenty of daylight to see what you are gathering. I would caution against harvesting your plant material at night. It does not add to the mystique to be skulking around in the dark. You could accidentally nip a finger or take the wrong plant while you are out there.

If you are out in the woods, wear long sleeves and long pants to protect yourself from bugs and assorted poison vines. Make sure you can identify poison oak, ivy, and sumac. They like to grow on trunks of trees. You don't want to become infected.

It can happen. A group of Master Gardeners went to clear deadwood out of a large area of flower beds in the park and didn't notice or identify that the wood was covered in poison ivy and poison oak vines. Needless to say, a few days later, they were all covered themselves as well. When I was told this story I started to laugh, only to be glared at by the still-rash-covered Master Gardeners. The point is, keep your eyes open. Be wise and work in harmony with nature, not against it . . . and try to avoid poison ivy if you can.

3

Won't you come into my garden?
I would like my roses to see you.

RICHARD SHERIDAN

❧

Flower Magick

If you're like me, you have a hard time passing by a flower—any flower—without stopping. Whether you are admiring the blooms as you stroll down a winding garden path, considering a display of perennials at a nursery, or being drawn to a clever arrangement of fresh flowers, you just can't help yourself. Do you find yourself compelled to stop, take a good whiff of the flower's aroma, or gently stroke the petals and coo over them? This generally indicates that you're a goner. Congratulations! You're going to have a blast performing flower magick.

Just for fun (yes, I do use that word a lot, don't I? That's okay, magick is supposed to be a joyous thing), you may want to ask yourself what your favorite type of gift flower is. It will give you a little insight on yourself, and you might be surprised by what the answer can mean.

Is the rose your favorite bloom to give or receive? Then you're a romantic, traditional and tasteful. If you love the spicy scent of carnations, then you are a nurturer, a caregiver, and have lots of energy. Do you have a thing for daisies? You have a cheerful, sunny outlook and are practical. The lily is your preference? You're sensual, luxurious, and enjoy having or making beautiful things. The orchid is your preferred flower? Well, then, you have impeccable taste, and have a hidden, exotic side to your personality.

Listing every correspondence for magickal herbs and flowers could fill up an entire book, and has. The herbal works of the late Scott Cunningham are required reading if you are serious about expanding your knowledge of natural magick. Cunningham left us a legacy of herbal information that is both detailed and comprehensive. That's a tough combination to beat, and I am certainly not going to try.

What I would like to do is give you an elementary list of floral correspondences, and some suggestions for easy-to-grow magickal flowers and blooming herbs. Color floral magick is a uncomplicated way to get in there and start working garden witchery. You should be familiar with color correspondence charts by now. Right?

I cannot stress enough how important it is for you to experiment with your own color correspondences. Working with flower magick is a very individual process. Your experience counts. Go with what works for you. Case in point: For some witches, blue is the healing color, not red. If you always have had success with blue as a healing color, I am certainly not going to tell you that you're wrong.

The following information is to be used as a springboard to get you thinking, and then to add ideas of your own to. As you work through this chapter, start making notes on your favorite flowers and their magickal correlations (use the journal in the back of this book!). List the flowers that you would like to try your hand at growing in your own garden and check on the meanings of those that are already growing at home.

Please note that some floral colors, like blue, green, and the black/burgundy pigment, can be a challenge to find. There are very few true green or black flowers, but they are available. If you imagine black flowers as gothic and/or macabre, think of it this way instead. Black flowers in the garden make a contribution that goes beyond novelty or shock value, for they are unequaled at providing contrast. Another excellent point to make is that most of the "black" flowers aren't really black at all. In actuality they are very dark purple, red, or brown. Here are a few suggestions for some stylish, black-colored flowers for your garden.

If you are into irises, try Black Swan (zones 3–10). It was introduced in 1960 and is a reliable blooming garden plant that will add a little mystery to your borders. There are also black hollyhocks, an heirloom variety called Nigra (*Alcea rosea*), hardy from zones 2–10. Look for the new dark burgundy cosmos. There is a sultry maroon-black tulip called Queen of the Night (zones 3–8). Imagine this tulip underplanted with white daffodils or blue forget-me-nots (underplanting is simply planting a shorter flower at the base of a taller one. This may help hide longer stems and it gives the flowers a thicker, more "plumped up" look).

A few varieties of roses are so dark burgundy that they have a black cast to them. Watch for the moss rose Nuits de Young (zones 5–10). This shrubby rose has thornless stems. Instead, its stems are covered with a dark, prickly moss. It grows four to five feet tall, blooms only once a year during midsummer, and possesses some of the darkest flowers of any rose.

I have easily located black pansies such as *Viola* Black Magic (zones 5–10) in my hometown. There is also another pansy variety available in the fall months called Trick-or-Treat (zones 5–10). These colorful seasonal pansies are a mixture of solid black, bright orange, and deep purple. They are great for pumping up the color in your fall garden, and for dressing up containers and window boxes, just in time for Halloween.

Now, on to a more elusive flower color: green. Are there really any green flowers, you may wonder? Check out the flowers on Bells of Ireland, they are green. So is a species or two of miniature rose. A few daffodil and tulip varieties are a pale green and white mixture. If nothing else is available, you can always use herb foliage, hosta leaves, or ferns.

As for blue, you have more options. Most of the true blue flowers are sacred to Venus, such as the morning glory and tall delphiniums. Delphiniums, a great perennial for the back of the garden, come in several shades of blue. Another fun garden perennial is the star-shaped balloon flower (*Platycodon grandiflorum*). Kids love them. They look like blue balloons before they pop open. More options include pastel blue pansies. These are readily available in the spring and fall. For a lavender-blue, try iris, and hybrid tea roses such as Blue Girl.

You'll figure it out. Look in seed and plant catalogs for more unusual floral colors and varieties. If you find yourself reading this list of flower colors and magickal correspondences and automatically thinking of flowers to fill the roles, good for you!

FLOWER COLORS AND MAGICKAL CORRESPONDENCES

WHITE: The Maiden, all purpose, purification, protection, and moon magick

GREEN: The God, element of earth, faeries, healing, money, luck, and fertility

PINK: Friendship, children, affection, and love

RED: The Mother, element of fire, lust, love, sex, healing, and protection

YELLOW: Element of air, wisdom, mental powers, and divination

ORANGE: Energy, vitality, and success

PURPLE: Power, psychic abilities, and passion

BLUE: Element of water, healing, sleep, and peace

BROWN AND BEIGE: Home, stability, and pets

BLACK AND DARK BURGUNDY: The Crone, banishing, breaking hexes, and removing negativity

> *Flowers always make people better,*
> *happier, and more helpful;*
> *they are sunshine, food*
> *and medicine to the soul.*
> LUTHER BURBANK

Flowers of the Month

Another correspondence that you have available to you are the flowers of your birth month. These flowers, like your birth stone, are assigned to specific months of the year. Working with the flower of your birth month is a great way to put some extra kick into any garden witchery that you do. Try it for yourself. Keep track of your results in your garden witchery journal.

The month of January has the carnation and the snowdrop. The carnation, as mentioned earlier, bestows energy and healing. The snowdrop, the flower of late winter and early spring, symbolizes new beginnings.

February birthdays can claim the violet and the primrose. The humble violet, found most often growing in your lawn, is a faery flower and is used for love and protection. The primrose blooms in early spring. Magickal uses are protection and love. In England, gardeners looking for signs of spring anticipate the first primroses the way Americans watch for the earliest daffodils.

To March belongs the daffodil. You know spring has arrived when the daffodils start to bloom. Magickally used for fertility and love, this favorite spring bulb needs to be planted in the fall. Daffodils are a traditional flower for the festival of Ostara, the spring equinox.

April has the sweet pea, the daisy, and the lily. The sweet pea is used for friendship and strength. The daisy and lily are both faery favorites. The daisy symbolizes love. The lily is employed in the breaking of love spells. When lilies are planted in the garden, they keep both ghosts and sinister influences away from your home. The white lily is a symbol for the archangel Gabriel.

May birthdays have lily of the valley and the hawthorn. Once again, both of these are attractive to the faeries. The lily of the valley has been cultivated for over four hundred years, and is a popular bridal flower due to its fragrance. While lily of the valley is magickally used to perk you up and lift your spirits, all parts of the plant are mildly toxic and should not be ingested. The blooms of the hawthorn are used in spells for fertility, happiness, and good luck in fishing.

Born in the month of June? You claim the rose and the honeysuckle. Roses are primarily used for love, but have many other uses, depending on the color of the bloom (see chapter 1). The petals may be used in other magickal mixtures to help speed things up. Honeysuckle is for prosperity spells. Bring some blooming honeysuckle into your house to attract money.

July birthdays have the larkspur and water lily. The larkspur is the common name for delphinium. The larkspur, sacred to Venus, is used for health and protection. Water lilies fall in the category of water plants. Use them in rituals that involve the element of water, such as healings, emotions, and psychic powers.

Folks that are born in the month of August have the gladiola and poppy. The gladiola is a tall, stalky, intensely scented flower that is used by florists in large funeral arrangements. I would employ this flower as a tool for ending relationships or situations that you have outgrown, as in a "my old way of life has died, it's time for me to move on in a more positive way" kind of thing. On a more upbeat note, the poppy is used for luck and prosperity. The poppy is sacred to many Greek/Roman deities, including one of my favorites, Demeter, the goddess of the harvest.

September babies have the morning glory and the aster. The morning glory blooms in September and the vines can be used in binding spells. When grown in the garden, it brings peace and happiness. The aster, a butterfly favorite, was sacred to all the Greek gods and is used primarily for love spells.

Was October when you made your debut? You've got the calendula and cosmos. Calendulas have the planetary association of the sun. Use them for strength, healing, and justice. Cosmos, most often grown as an annual, are bright, sunny little flowers that come in a wide variety of colors and heights. Refer to the magickal flower color chart on page 11 for the associations. (Ha! Have to figure this one out for yourselves!)

To the month of November goes the chrysanthemum. The magical power of protection is the gift of this flower. Its elemental correspondence is fire. Here is another flower that, when grown in your yard, is supposed to protect you from ghosts. Considering that Samhain, famous for its free-roaming spirits, just ended, that's pretty appropriate.

December, the final month of the calendar year, has holly, ivy, and the poinsettia. The magickal pair of holly and ivy is classically used at Yule for seasonal decorations, the holly being the male plant, and the ivy the female. Holly is used for protection and ivy is used for fidelity and love. The poinsettia, a traditional holiday flower, came to us from Mexico. Another toxic houseplant, keep poinsettias away from pets and small children who might try to eat it. Poinsettia corresponds with the Lady of Guadalupe, also known as the Mother of the Americas. Her sacred day is December 12.

> *What was paradise? But a garden,*
> *an orchard of trees and herbs,*
> *full of pleasure, and nothing there but delights.*
> CHARLES DUDLEY WARNER

Flowering Herbs of the Magickal Garden

So far, we have covered floral color correspondences and looked at the flowers of the month. Now we return to your backyard gardens, or front yard gardens, as the case may be. I have listed plants that I feel are fairly uncomplicated to grow and easy to obtain from your local nurseries. If you are new to gardening, give yourself a break and start small. You can always expand the garden and grow more varieties in a few seasons. Remember that gardening isn't learned in one summer. It takes years. You are probably going to lose a few plants (I have) and make some mistakes.

Perennials take about three seasons to become mature. Keep that in mind when you plant that little baby perennial in your garden. If the identification tag says plant them eighteen inches apart, do so. It's going to grow. If you mess up and plant them too close together, you can always move them farther apart later if you have to. You'll learn as you go along, just like the rest of us gardeners.

The following is a list of a witch's dozen (that's thirteen) easy-to-grow magickal flowering herbs for most gardens. The common name is followed by the botanical name, which appears in italics. The plant's magickal correspondence is given immediately afterward.

I have also included something that is missing from most magickal texts: practical tips, the plant's growth habits, soil conditions, and approximate bloom times. In general, I have noticed that perennials that bloom prior to the summer solstice have a shorter bloom period than those that bloom after the solstice. The reason? Once the length of the sunlight hours has peaked, the growing cycle loses its urgency and flowering lasts for a longer period of time.

A Witch's Dozen of Flowering Magickal Herbs

BERGAMOT OR BEE BALM (*Monarda*) is used for prosperity and success. This orangy-mint scent is clean and refreshing. The flowers may be used in floral arrangements, either fresh or dried. This aromatic herb's leaves and blooms are used both in potpourri and teas. Cultivated in sun or shade, this aggressive perennial is attractive to butterflies and bees. To keep it under control, divide the plant at least every third year, discarding the dead center. Zones 4–9.

CONEFLOWERS (*Echinacea*) strengthen spells. This perennial is a good choice for a beginning gardener. Coneflowers grow over three feet tall in full sun. They will also grow successfully in part shade, but they will not reach the same height as those grown in the sun. Coneflowers are native plants to most of the Midwest. They tolerate drought conditions, poor soils, multiply readily, and transplant well. Plan on dividing these every third year. Coneflowers make superb cut flowers. Birds and butterflies love them. Butterflies will use them as landing pads. Goldfinches raid them in the fall for the thistle, when the blooms have all faded and the thistles have dried. So don't cut them back, let the birds have them. Available in purple and white varieties, a popular white variety is called White Swan. In zone 5, where I live, the coneflower starts to bloom in late June and continues through October. Zones 3–9.

CINQUEFOIL (*Potentilla*), also known as five-finger grass—the five points of the leaves stand for love, riches, good health, power, and knowledge. This herb is most often employed in money spells. Cinquefoil grows in sun to part shade and isn't too finicky about soils. It is a compact plant that blooms in June and July. The height of the plant depends on the variety. A tough, non-fussy variety that I grow in my garden has peachy-coral colored blooms. This variety is called Miss Willmott and grows eighteen inches tall. When the blooms fade, dead-head them and enjoy the foliage that stays in neat green mounds. Zones 4–8.

FEVERFEW (*Chrysanthemum parthenium*). A flower known to herbalists for centuries, who use it for health, protection, and to guard against accidents. Eating a few leaves of fresh feverfew every day—for example, on a sandwich—is supposed to alleviate migraine headaches. Feverfew grows well in the sun and likes drier soil conditions. Bloom time is around midsummer. The blooms of the feverfew are the bonus of growing this herb. The small, open clusters of tiny, daisylike flowers make great filler for arrangements.

Don't be afraid to clip a lot of blooms for yourself to enjoy, after the plant is established. If you do not dead-head this herb, those seeds will scatter and you'll have it everywhere. (Hooray! Free plants!) If you choose to dry feverfew, be careful handling those blooms when they dry, as they are fragile. After this plant establishes itself in your garden, probably in its second or third growing season, divide it up in autumn. Zones 4–7.

HENS AND CHICKS (*Sempervivum tectorum*), a.k.a. houseleek. Ancient Romans grew this plant, which was rumored to be a gift from the God Jupiter. Legend says the plant prevents your home from being struck by lightning. This herb bestows protection and it guards against fire—sort of a magickal fire insurance policy. It keeps away evil spirits and repels black magick. Hens and chicks prefer sunny gardens and dry, well-drained soil. They also grow well in strawberry pots and containers on a sunny patio. Hens and chicks send off small rosettes that develop roots and become separate plants. Grown for its succulent type of foliage, this plant was once used as a first-aid plant, much as we use aloe vera today. If grown in the garden, it will survive most winters. If, however, your winter temperatures are extreme and you have hens and chicks planted in a container, move them indoors as a houseplant. Zones 4–8.

HYSSOP (*Hyssopus officinalis*). This herb is used for cleansings. Harvest the flowering tops and newer leaves. These may be added into a ritual bath or used in charm bags tucked around the house to protect your home. Hyssop is a fragrant herb and may be added to potpourri mixtures. Hyssop prefers light, well-drained, alkaline soils. It may grow eighteen inches to three feet tall, depending on the variety, and likes full sun. Zones 5–9.

LARKSPUR (*Delphinium*) has the magical correspondences of health and protection. Larkspur is a tall border plant available in white and different shades of blue. They can be grown as an annual or perennial. These pretty flowers are great for arrangements and add color in potpourri mixes. Larkspur grows anywhere from two to four feet tall and usually needs to be staked as it grows. It prefers moist, fertile soil and likes full sun. Bloom time is usually late spring to early summer. Perennial larkspur grows best in milder summer climates. Zones 3–7.

I have a love-hate relationship with larkspur. I adore those blue flowers but I have a tough time growing larkspur successfully in my garden. So, I grow it as an annual . . . a short-lived annual. As soon as the heat and humidity of a Missouri summer hits, mine dies.

LAVENDER (*Lavandula angustifolia*) is used in love spells, calming charm bags, and dream pillows. The scent of lavender is cleansing, peaceful, and may be employed to calm headaches. A few fresh stems of blooming lavender or a drop or two of the essential oil in your bath water will help you wind down after a tough day. Perennial Munstead lavender grows twelve to eighteen inches tall. It is drought tolerant and appreciates sandy soil (zones 5–9). Lavender thrives in sunny, hot conditions, like along a sidewalk or a driveway. Harvest lavender as the blooms just start to open. If you dead-head your lavender, it will bloom several times throughout the growing season. There are many varieties of lavender. Make sure when you choose one that you are buying a variety that will winter over in your climate. (Check the tags for zone information; look for the word "perennial." If it says "tender perennial," then I would say it wouldn't survive cold winter climates.)

PEONY (*Paeonia officinalis*). Used for its protective abilities, the peony bloom may be worn for this reason. Arrange the blooms in a vase in your home to prevent nightmares. Plant the shrub in the garden to protect your property. Peonies come in a wide variety of colors, including yellow. Peonies take a few years to become established, but they are well worth the wait. A fragrant May bloomer, it reminds me of old-style cabbage roses. Peonies like their soil enriched with compost and are happy growing in full sun. The shrubs grow two to three feet tall and need to be staked as they grow. Zones 3–8.

A good trick is to take old tomato cages and, as the peonies break the ground in the spring, train the shoots to grow up inside of the cages. Plan on two to three cages per peony bush. As the foliage fills out, the cages become invisible. Dead-head the faded blooms and, later in autumn, cut the withered and brown foliage back to an inch or two from the ground. Store the cages away for next year.

SUNFLOWER (*Helianthus annuus*). This annual flower, cultivated by the Native Americans thousands of years ago, has always been honored as a symbol of the sun. Magickal uses are truth, fertility, and wishes. Sleeping with a sunflower beneath your pillow will tell you the truth of any matter. These plants require full sun and are easily started from seed. Sunflowers are heavy feeders, meaning they need lots of fertilizer. The height of sunflowers can vary, depending on the variety, from two feet to ten feet tall, and they are now available in many colors and bloom times. Check your seed packet for variety-specific bloom times, usually late July through September. Sunflowers will not winter over, but you may save some of the seeds and plant them again next season if you wish.

Birds love sunflowers. If you grow the large-headed variety, save a seed head or two and put it out in the winter for the birds to snack on.

TANSY (*Tanacetum vulgare*). Tansy's magickal uses are for health and a long life. It is a faery plant that has the folk name of buttons. Tansy grows anywhere, in just about any type of soil. A variety that I have is fern leaf tansy. It grows two feet tall and is aggressive. (That's a nice way for gardeners to say it spreads like crazy!) They bloom in late summer to early fall and the foliage is strongly scented. The blooms look like little golden buttons, hence the folk name. The dried flowers hold their color fairly well. You may try growing tansy near fruit trees to repel insects. The flowers are used to make yellow dye. Zones 5–8.

WOOLY BETONY (*Stachys byzantina*), a.k.a. lamb's ears. Magickal uses for lamb's ears include protection, to repel nightmares, for healing, and for use in children's magick. Dried and crumbled lamb's ears sprinkled around the parameter of your home forms a protective barrier that no negativity or evil can pass. Lamb's ears are easy to grow. This is a perennial that can grow even in poor soils, sun or shade. A lovely, soft, fuzzy border plant grown for its silver foliage, it's a great plant for a children's garden. Kids love to pet lamb's ears. Bloom time is July—the blooms are a rich purple and the bloom stalks grow about two feet tall. If you want to keep them as only a border plant, cut off the bloom stalks as they appear. I happen to like the blooms. After the blooms have faded, I usually start to control the size of the plant by dividing it, as it is very aggressive.

With one plant that I bought seven years ago I now have lamb's ears in all of my beds— and in my neighbors' too! (I gave lots of it away.) Don't be afraid to pull this one up if it gets too big. Pull up unwanted sections (it spreads by underground shoots) until you have a size you can live with. Transplant those around your yard or pot it up and share it with your neighbors. Remember, it will expand out again next year, that's what makes it fun. Zones 4–8.

YARROW (*Achillea*). An all-purpose magickal herb, often called the witch's herb, yarrow instills courage, strength, love, and friendship, and banishes evil. It is a faery plant. Yarrow is one of my favorite perennial herbs. A variety that I grow in my gardens is Moonshine, a golden-yellow yarrow that dries beautifully. Yarrow is great for fresh arrangements. It is available in white, yellow, and shades of red and pink.

Harvest these blooms when they are looking their best. Band them together, cover with a brown paper bag, and hang them upside down to dry in a non-humid, well-ventilated room. See chapter 8 for a yarrow love charm. Yarrow prefers full sun and likes rich, moist soil. The bloom time starts in late May to early June. The blooms last on the plants for almost six weeks. If you dead-head them after they have faded, you will be rewarded with another small batch of flowers in late summer. Zones 4–8.

4

Come forth into the light of things,
let nature be your teacher.
WILLIAM WORDSWORTH

Florigraphy and Flower Folklore

The magick and folklore of flowers is a fascinating subject. An old term once used to describe the secret knowledge of the magickal properties of herbs, plants, and flowers is wort-cunning. "Wort" is an old English word for herb, and "cunning" is a synonym for craft. Therefore, the meaning of wort-cunning becomes crystal clear: herb craft.

The wisewomen and cunning men of the past knew the ways of spellweaving and herbal magicks, the correct time to plant and harvest the crops, the interpretations of weather signs, and the omens of animals in the wilderness around them. In an age where your family could live or die depending on how well your crops grew and how successfully you hunted and gathered, this was essential information.

This earthy wisdom was doubtless handed down through the family, from mother to daughter and father to son. Their inheritance is fruitful indeed. This practical knowledge of herbal magick and agricultural information was filtered down throughout the years as plant folklore, innocent charms, weather lore, home remedies, and country superstitions.

Enter the modern witch. You just know that the real earth magick and herbal knowledge is out there somewhere, if only you could find someone to teach you. Wait a minute. Try looking a little closer to home. Have you tried your grandparents? Ask them about old superstitions, cures, and home remedies that their parents used.

If you have an experienced gardener in the family, go make nice. Some of the best practical advice for gardening, along with plant folklore, that I have ever learned came innocently enough from a senior citizen. Go join a garden club or attend a free lecture, and sit and absorb some useful garden information. Behave yourself, now, and don't scare the hell out of anyone by dropping your magickal interests into the conversation or by whipping out your latest Craft book. Not only is that bad manners, it won't get you anywhere at all. Be discreet.

You are going to have to dig deep and do your homework. A good place to start is by taking a long, hard look at old superstitions and folklore. Hit the library and see what you can find. A clever little trick is to start by researching mythology, plant folklore, and florigraphy.

Florigraphy is known as the language of flowers. During the Victorian era, people often utilized flowers to declare their feelings. A romantic and "secret" way to communicate with members of the opposite sex, this custom developed into a language of flowers. This floral language was based on the traditions of older mythology and folklore.

There are many different modern versions of florigraphy to choose from. However, I wanted something with a little history. While researching this subject I came across several lists, all of which had been published in the late 1800s. By far, my most interesting find was an antique, massive "floral vocabulary" that was noted in the back of a modern-day gardening book, published about ten years ago. The modern author credited his source as belonging to a Miss Mary M. Griffin, from her book *Drops from Flora's Cup*. My curiosity was piqued.

The full title of the book is *Drops from Flora's Cup, or the Poetry of Flowers*. Published in Boston by G. W. Cottrell and Company, in the year 1845, Miss Griffin's book is considered rare by both the author who perpetuated her work and the main branch of the St. Louis Public Library. As of the spring of 2001, there were no copies of it available within Missouri's library systems. They could confirm that the book did indeed exist and that at one time the library did have a copy of it. Unfortunately, that might have been as long as over one hundred years ago.

This sent me on a quest for other antique "language of the flowers" lists. But where to find them? I contacted the Missouri Botanical Garden's library and hit paydirt. The gracious ladies who work there informed me that they had at least thirteen books on the subject, many dating from Victorian times. The books were not available to check out, however they did have a copy machine. Was I interested? I assured them that I was. As soon as our work schedules permitted, my husband and I coordinated our days off and drove into the city to see what we could find.

We spent some interesting hours at the botanical library. You'd be amazed at what you discover when you look hard enough. There is older information on folklore and magick. Contrary to what you may have been told, you *can* uncover interesting magickal folklore that was published before the 1980s. Yes, sometimes it is over-romanticized or prejudiced, but it is there. I feel that a good-natured warning is appropriate here. When searching through antique books, you need to keep your sense of humor handy. You will need it.

During the time period of the mid to late 1800s, the Druids, it seems, were looked upon as noble, romantic figures, while witches were considered thoroughly evil. (No big surprise there.) When I found an entire chapter dedicated to plants used by witches in their "cruel sorcery," not to mention their "nefarious trade," I grumbled and hissed.

Nefarious trade? Oh, please . . . My husband just grinned at me, quietly made a rude remark, and made me laugh. Still, we kept researching. I took many notes and found some interesting information on faeries, weather lore, and floral love charms.

Many of the flower folklore books at the botanical library were indeed over 120 years old and fragile. Filled with the fanciful style of poetry that was popular at the time and some beautiful color plates of botanical drawings, what I would have given for a color copier! A few of the books that had floral languages matched up word for word with Mary Griffin's. It is interesting to note that these books had been published approximately twenty to forty years *later* than Griffin's.

I believe that Miss Griffin's work deserves to see the light of day once again. Her original floral vocabulary is immense, and many of the plants are difficult to find. Listed below are some highlights of the more familiar plants. From Mary M. Griffin's *Drops from Flora's Cup*, in the language of the period (1845).

MISS MARY'S FLORAL VOCABULARY

ALLYSUM: Worth beyond beauty

ANGELICA: Inspiration

ASTER: Beauty in retirement

BACHELOR'S BUTTON: Hope in misery

BETONY (LAMB'S EAR): Surprise

BLUEBELL: Constancy

BUTTERCUP: Ingratitude

CHAMOMILE: Energy in adversity

CHRYSANTHEMUM: Cheerfulness

CLEMATIS: Mental beauty

COLUMBINE: Folly

COREOPSIS: Ever cheerful

DAFFODIL: Delusive hope

DAISY: Innocence

DAHLIA: Dignity and elegance

DANDELION: Oracle

DOGWOOD: Durability

ELDER: Compassion

ELM: Dignity

FERN: Symmetry

FENNEL: Strength

FORGET-ME-NOT: True love

FOXGLOVE: I am ambitious for your sake

FUCHSIA: Confiding love

GERANIUM, ROSE: Preference

GERANIUM, SCARLET: Consolation

HEARTSEASE (PANSY): Think of me

HELIOTROPE: Devotion

HONEYSUCKLE: Bonds of love

ICE PLANT: Your looks freeze me

IRIS: A message for you

IVY: Friendship

JASMINE, WHITE: Amiability

JASMINE, YELLOW: Elegant gracefulness

LARKSPUR: Fickleness

LAVENDER: Acknowledgment

LILAC: First emotion of love

LILY OF THE VALLEY: Return of happiness

LILY, WHITE: Purity and modesty

LOVE-IN-A-MIST: Perplexity

MAGNOLIA: Love of nature

MARIGOLD: Inquietude

MIMOSA: Sensitiveness

PEONY: Ostentation

PERIWINKLE: Sweet remembrances

PHLOX: We are united

PRIMROSE, PINK: I am more constant than thou

ROSEMARY: Remembrance

ROSE: Beauty

SAGE: Domestic virtues

SNAPDRAGON: Presumption

TANSY: Resistance

THISTLE: I will never forget thee

THYME: Activity

TULIP: Declaration of love

VERBENA: Sensibility

VIOLET, BLUE: Modesty

VIOLET, WHITE: Candor

WITCH HAZEL: A spell

YARROW: Thou alone canst cure

ZINNIA: Absence

A kiss of the sun for pardon,
The song of the birds for mirth,
One is nearer God's heart in a garden
Than anywhere else on earth.

DOROTHY FRANCES GURNEY

Cottage Flower Folklore

Old cottage gardens were thickly planted with flowers and herbs, not only for their appearance but for their magickal properties. Part of the tradition and mystique of the wise-woman was her cottage garden stuffed full of aromatic and mysterious herbs and plants. Old-fashioned, romantic, and a reminder of less-complicated times, cottage-style gardens are once again becoming popular.

Forget the slick, modern, and formal garden. A cottage garden places the emphasis on comfort and easy maintenance. There are no hard and fast rules on plant arrangement and color combinations in cottage gardening. Do you like orange marigolds and purple petunias together? Go ahead. Plant some silvery betony (lamb's ears) with them as a neutral blending color and enjoy. A cottage garden offers a miscellany of plants, all with different heights, colors, textures, and bloom times. Vegetables, flowers, and herbs may be grown together in a whimsical arrangement. The more the merrier!

A cottage garden can be any size and shape. Think of an enchanted garden, complete with ivied walls and old clay pots overflowing with flowers . . . rustic privacy fences for seclusion or charming white picket fences to frame the garden . . . trellises and arbors that support climbing roses, clematis, and morning glories . . . a bird bath for the songbirds to splash about in, and . . . oops! Sorry, I got carried away. Back to cottage garden flowers.

When choosing plants for your new cottage garden, or for pumping up your established garden, look for easy-to-grow varieties. Be sure to add wildflowers that are native to your area, such as California poppies for the West Coast or purple coneflowers for the Midwest.

Roses in cottage gardens are traditional. If you're leery of growing roses, consider English or Rugosa roses for a low-maintenance rose. Usually disease resistant, they require no spraying and are more cold hardy than fussier hybrid teas. Rugosa and some varieties of English roses may only bloom once per season; however, they are carefree and their blooms are very old-fashioned.

The symbolism of cottage garden flowers can be a useful tool for the garden witch. Growing a magickal garden is easy if we know something of the old flower folklore. Refer to this list of blooming shrubs, garden plants, and flowers as you design spells of your own creation. You may care to coordinate these flowers with color magick for an extra boost. This fragrant vocabulary may include the following nostalgic favorites.

> *"We can talk," said the Tiger-lily,*
> *"when there's anybody worth talking to."*
>
> LEWIS CARROLL,
> *THROUGH THE LOOKING GLASS* (1871)

The Language of Cottage Flowers

ALYSSUM: Sweet purity

APPLE BLOSSOM: Beauty and goodness

ASTILBE: Earthly pleasures

AZALEA, WHITE: First love

BALLOON FLOWER: Faraway friends

BEGONIA: Premonition

BLACK-EYED SUSAN: Fairness

BLEEDING HEART: Brokenhearted

BEE BALM: Irresistible

BRIDAL WREATH SPIREA: Victory

BUTTERFLY BUSH: Wantonness

CALADIUM: Joy

CARNATION, PINK: Encouragement

CARNATION, RED: Passion

CARNATION, WHITE: Pure devotion

CINQUEFOIL: Beloved daughter

COCKSCOMB: Humor

CONEFLOWER, PURPLE: Skill and resilience

CORAL BELLS: Study and hard work

CREPE MYRTLE: Eloquence

DAYLILY: Siren

DUSTY MILLER: Respected grandmother

ENCHANTER'S NIGHTSHADE: Witchcraft

EVENING PRIMROSE: Humble devotion

EVERLASTING FLOWER: Death of hope

FERN: Tempestuous passion

FEVERFEW: Protection

FLOWERING ALMOND: Hope

FORSYTHIA: Good nature

HOLLYHOCK: Enthusiasm and zeal

HOSTA: Devotion

HYDRANGEA: Moodiness

IMPATIENS: Speed

LAMB'S EAR: Support

LAVENDER: Distrust

LEMON BALM: Health

LUPIN: Overassertiveness

MEADOWSWEET: Lovely bride

MOCK ORANGE: Virgin bride

MORNING GLORY: Greet the new day

NIGELLA: Kiss me

PANSY, PURPLE: Happy memories

PINKS (DIANTHUS): Forever lovely

PLUM (BLOSSOMS): Fertility

PUSSY WILLOW: Friendship

QUEEN ANNE'S LACE: Return home

QUINCE: Temptation

ROSE: Love

SANTOLINA: Protection from harm

SEDUM: Peace

SUNFLOWER: Royalty

SWEET PEA: Tenderness

SWEET WOODRUFF: Eternal life

TANSY: Safe pregnancy

TIGER LILY: Erotic love

TRUMPET FLOWER: Fiery passion

VERBENA: Spellbound

VERVAIN: Witchcraft

WEIGELA (BLOOM): A heart
    that's true

YARROW: Witch's herb

ZINNIA: Faraway friends

I met a Lady in the Meads
Full beautiful, a fairy's child
Her hair was long, her foot was light
And her eyes were wild—

KEATS

Flowers for the Lady: Goddesses and Associated Plants

If you are calling on a particular goddess, it certainly doesn't hurt to have as many things in sympathy with her as you can find. I have found that the Lady seems to appreciate the extra work and thoughtfulness of the gesture. Most modern magickal books have a candle and color correspondence chart, and the text will tell you what lunar associations the goddesses have. But what about plant, flower, and even fruit correspondences for the ladies? Those are harder to find. Never fear, I've got some for you.

In keeping with our backyard magick, these everyday plants are easy to obtain. The fruit shouldn't be any more difficult to produce (sorry, bad pun) than a trip to the grocery store. If you have trouble locating vervain, try growing annual flowering verbena—you may use those brightly colored blooms as a substitute.

ARADIA: Rue, vervain/verbena, and apple

ARTEMIS: Artemesia, daisy, and cypress

ASTRAEA: Aster, Michaelmas daisy

BAST: Catnip

BRIGHID OR BRIDE: Dandelion, crocus, helebores, and blackberries

CERRIDWEN: Vervain/verbena

DEMETER OR CERES: Red poppy, wheat

DIANA: Apple, rue, and rose

FREYA: Maidenhair fern, daisy, rose, primrose, and strawberries

HATHOR: Rose, grapes

HECATE: Cyclamen, willow, and monkshood (aconite)

HERA: Iris, willow, and apples

HOLDA: Rose in full bloom

IRIS (Greek goddess of the rainbow): Iris (in all colors), rose

ISIS: Rose, heather, and purple iris

LADY OF GUADALUPE: Red and pink roses, poinsettias

LILITH: Lily; deep-red, thorny, garden-style roses; and the willow

MINERVA: Thistle, olive, and mulberries

NEPHTHYS: Lily

PERSEPHONE: Parsley, pomegranate

SELENE: Rose, bluebell, nicotiana, and all white and night-blooming flowers

VENUS OR APHRODITE: Violet, morning glory, rose, and all true blue flowers

> *The more simple we are,*
> *the more complete we become.*
> AUGUST RODIN

Flower Fascinations: The Art of Simpling

Fascination is defined as "to bewitch and hold spellbound by an irresistible power." Flower fascinations are elementary flower spells and charms for various magickal uses.

A *simple* is described as a medicine plant. A simple is also known as a basic element, having only one ingredient, such as a flower or an herb. The yarrow love charm in chapter 8 is one example of a simple. The art of simpling consists of working with select magickal herbs and flowers. You can sew them up into charm bags, or fashion flowers, foliage, and herbs into a small enchanted bouquet, or posy.

Working within the legacy of the folklore of plants, you can create your own simples and flower fascinations. Try herbs for protection and prosperity, or flowers for love and healing.

These flower fascinations and charms, of my own design, were inspired by my research into the 1800s flower folklore. Work these enchantments with positive intentions and they will make you smile. Basically, these are fun, fast, and—dare I say it?—simple.

A SMALL NOSEGAY of lily of the valley, bleeding hearts, and violets, arranged in a tiny jar, will bestow blessings from the faeries and help cheer you up after a hard day at work. Tie the flowers up with a white satin ribbon, and breathe in the scent! (All of these flowers should be blooming at the same time in your garden, late April through early May.) My daughter calls these miniature flower arrangements "faery bouquets."

> *Faery posy of white, pink, and blue*
>
> *Help me out here, my boss is a shrew.*
>
> *Safe now at home, I'm so glad to be*
>
> *Rid me of anger and negativity.*

WALKING AROUND A BLOOMING SNAPDRAGON three times in a widdershins (counterclockwise) direction is thought to cure you of any bewitchment. Likewise, a few stems of snapdragons in a vase will help to protect you from manipulative intentions.

AN ARCHAIC EXAMPLE OF A SIMPLE is to place snapdragon seeds inside of a small blue linen bag and wear the bag around your neck. This will prevent any negative energy from affecting you. Nowadays, tuck the little bag in your pocket or purse. Try this charm to go along with it.

> *Snapdragon seeds in a pouch of blue,*
>
> *I request your magick, my need is true.*

Now protect me from hatred, send evil away,

Lord and Lady, bless and guide me each day.

HELIOTROPE has the folk name of "cherry pie," and was thought to grant the power of invisibility. If you plant this herb in the garden close to the area where you perform magick, it will help you to keep a low magickal profile. Your discreet magickal actions should pass unnoticed by those curious neighbors or your in-laws. (Of course, if you are lighting a huge bonfire and the coven is dancing around the backyard skyclad on Friday nights, I don't know how effective this will be.) Ahem. Anyway, try planting this perennial in the waning moon. As you add this herb to your gardens, intone the following:

Heliotrope was called cherry pie,

Help shield my magick from mundane eyes.

By the dark of the moon and power of the sun,

Grant me privacy and peace, an' let it harm none.

A DECORATIVE BROOM adorned with ribbons, dried yarrow, and rosemary would be a excellent gift for a wedding or a handfasting. The herb yarrow was thought to have the power to keep a couple happily together for seven years. Rosemary signifies faithfulness and remembrance.

PLACE A CLOVER in your lover's shoe before they leave on a trip, and they will remain faithful during their absence.

CARRY THE FLOWERS OF THE BLUE BACHELOR'S BUTTONS in your pocket to draw success in love. (This is another example of a Venus flower hard at work.)

KEEPING A FEW ACORNS in your pocket is a charm for fertility, love, and attraction.

A BLOOMING REDBUD TREE contains great magick. In areas of the Ozarks, it was once thought that to cut branches off a redbud while the tree was in bloom would call down extreme bad luck on yourself. Instead, try tying a ribbon on a blossoming branch as you make a wish.

OAK OR ROWAN TWIGS bound together with red thread into a solar cross or a pentagram will make a mighty protective talisman for the home, car, or in your desk or locker at work. I adapted this modern charm from an old English rhyme.

> *Oaken/Rowan twigs and strings of red,*
>
> *Deflect all harm, gossip, and dread.*

THE LILAC is beloved by the faery kingdom. The fragrance of lilacs encourages clairvoyance and is a good aromatherapy scent for any type of psychic work. Try placing a vase of lilacs on your altar and repeat the following charm.

> *Fragrant lilac blooms are purple in hue,*
>
> *The gift of second sight this scent grants you.*
>
> *Sacred to the faeries this forever shall be,*
>
> *Lady, open my heart and allow me to see.*

LILAC is a great fragrance to be used whether you are an old hand at the Tarot or trying to learn the cards for the first time. Lighting a purple, lilac-scented candle will also aid you in your psychic endeavors. It will help you to open up the third eye and receive psychic impressions more easily. Also, a drop or two of lilac oil in your bath water is a powerful way to clear yourself of any psychic residue that you may have picked up during the day.

LAVENDER counteracts the evil eye. A few drops of lavender oil in your bath water will help to protect you. Ditto for lavender-scented soaps, perfumes, and body lotions. Lavender planted in the garden will bring good luck to your family.

AN OLD CURE FOR BED-WETTING was to make a child smell a dandelion on Beltane. Then they would stop their bed-wetting for a year. This may explain the old folk name for dandelions ... are you ready? It's "Piss-a-bed"!

THERE IS AN OLD SCOTTISH CUSTOM of eating an apple on Samhain night while looking into the mirror. Legend says that you will see your true love reflected there. A Victorian Halloween card states the following verse:

> On Halloween look in the glass,
>
> Your future husband's face will pass.

A modern adaptation of this charm could include standing before the mirror at midnight on Samhain. This new charm will help you to recognize a future or potential love. Slice the apple crosswise to expose the star-shaped arrangement of seeds inside. Light a tealight candle and place the apple slices and the candle before the mirror. (Make sure the candle is in a safe place to burn. If you have to, place the tealight in a heatproof bowl or small cauldron.) At midnight, say the following charm three times:

> As this Samhain night rushes past,
>
> Reveal to me a love that shall last.
>
> May I know them when next we meet
>
> May our love be both strong and sweet.

Allow the candle to burn out and, the next morning, leave the apple pieces outside as an offering to the nature spirits. Pay attention and see who you "meet" within the next thirty days.

FLOWERS BLOOMING OUT OF SEASON are considered to be omens, such as violets blooming in the fall. As this old rhyme warns,

> *Flowers out of season, trouble without reason.*

BLUE GARDEN VERONICA has the folk name of speedwell. Use this perennial flower in posies and charm bags for healing and speedy recoveries.

WHEN FLOWER STALKS BEND, the Irish say that they are bowing to the Fae Queen, who is somewhere nearby.

GATHER FROM THE GARDEN A POSY (a posy is an old term for a nosegay or tussie-mussie) of snapdragons, mullein, betony, lavender, and dill. On the night of the full moon, as the moon rises in the east, present it to the Goddess Selene and request her magickal aid and protection. These magickal herbs tied together with red and white ribbons will safeguard you from harm and melancholy.

> *Snapdragons, mullein, betony, and dill,*
>
> *Protect me from harm, shield me from ill will.*
>
> *Lavender counteracts the evil eye,*
>
> *While Selene gives her blessing from on high.*

In Eastern lands they talk in flowers,
And they tell in a garland their love and cares;
Each blossom that blooms in their garden bowers,
On its leaves a mystic language bears.

JAMES G. PERCIVAL

Tussie-Mussies

Posies, nosegays, and tussie-mussies date back to the sixteenth century. These miniature, handheld bouquets are filled with aromatic herbs and flowers. Tussie-mussies were carried for protection against sickness and to disguise bad odors (hence the name "nosegay"), and to ward off evil spirits. These dainty "talking bouquets" became popular because they held hidden messages based on the symbolic meaning of the plants.

By incorporating the language of flowers and through selecting your blooms and foliage with care, you can create a powerful flower fascination—not bad for such a little bouquet. Apply some of that garden witch know-how and kick it up a few notches with floral color magick and by coordinating various colored blooms and ribbons for specific magickal intent. Here are a few ideas to get you started.

FIRST LOVE: A pink rosebud, white azalea blooms, hosta leaves, feverfew blossoms, and blue forget-me-nots. Add a few satin ribbons in baby blue and pink for a little extra color magick. The pink, white, and blue colors of the flowers and ribbons in this tussie-mussie invoke love, peace, and hope. The significance of the blooms are as follows: the pink rosebud brings an innocent love; the azalea is for a first love; hosta leaves are for devotion; the feverfew stands for protection; and the forget-me-nots conjure true love.

I DESIRE YOU: An orange rose, fern foliage, nigella (love-in-a-mist), bergamot blooms, and a tiger lily. Tie with red ribbons for desire and orange for energy and stamina. Hey, is it warm in here? Floral meanings are: vitality and energy from the orange rose; passion from the ferns; "kiss me" from the nigella; "you are irresistible" from the bergamot; and, finally, erotic love from the tiger lily.

GET WELL SOON: A yellow rose, golden yarrow, lemon balm leaves, daisies, and a spray of bachelor's buttons. Coordinate the color of the ribbons with the flowers or with your own chosen color for healing magick. Floral meanings are as follows: yellow rose for joy and happiness; yarrow blossoms for healing magick; lemon balm for freshness and health; daisies for cheerfulness; and bachelor's buttons for healing energies.

Before making a tussie-mussie, posy, or nosegay, consider its theme and select the ingredients for their appearance and symbolism. Take a look at all those floral language charts from earlier in this chapter. They will provide you with the information that you will need.

Start the arrangement with a larger central bloom such as a rose, peony, or geranium as a focal point. Then encircle it with contrasting flowers and foliage. Work out from the center in a circular pattern. Bind the stems with green florist's tape as you go, to keep the posy tight. Build up the layers and emphasize the outer rim with large-leafed herbs.

The fuzzy leaves from lady's mantle are excellent for this purpose, as are variegated ivy, hosta foliage, ferns, angelica's glossy leaves, and the leaves from the common violet.

Finish off the bouquet by tying the coordinating ribbons around the stems in a decorative bow. Nosegays should stay fresh in water for about seven days, and can be dried by hanging them upside down in a warm, well-ventilated, dark room.

If you would like to create a tussie-mussie for a gift or even venture planting an old-fashioned posy or tussie-mussie garden for yourself, check the Cottage Flower Chart on pages 55–57 for plant suggestions. You may also try working with and growing any of these other magickal plants. See also the garden layout illustration, page 69.

ANGELICA: Use the blooms, feathery leaves, and the seed pods for inspiration.

BAY: Tuck in a leaf or two for glory.

CAMPANULA: Also known as bellflower, those perky blue blossoms signify gratitude.

CHAMOMILE: Flowers and foliage for strength in difficult situations.

COREOPSIS: Those bright yellow flowers have the meaning of "always cheerful."

DAISY: For cheer and innocence.

ELDER: The blossoms signify zealousness, energy, and action.

FENNEL: Conveys strength.

FERN: For passion and faery magick.

FEVERFEW: Brings protection from illness. Incorporate both the ferny foliage and the tiny daisylike blooms.

FORGET-ME-NOT: Stands for true love. These lovely blue flowers soften the bouquet.

GERANIUM: A scarlet geranium for comfort, a pink geranium for love, and a white geranium for fertility. A geranium bloom makes another large, respectable central flower to build from.

GOLDEN MARJORAM: Means "blushes." Perfect for a young girl or a bride.

HYSSOP: Traditionally used since medieval times for cleanliness.

IVY: The leaves and tendrils stand for fidelity and love.

LADY'S MANTLE: Protection—use the fuzzy leaves for the outer leaves and the chartreuse flowers as fillers.

LEMON BALM: For sympathy and for a pick-me-up. A wonderful aromatic herb.

LINDEN BLOSSOM: For conjugal love.

MINTS: Mint is traditionally used to convey virtue. There are so many colors and scents of mint to choose from—chocolate, orange, pineapple . . .

PANSIES: A cure for the brokenhearted.

ROSEMARY: For remembrance. Work in the sprigs and blooming tops.

ROSEBUD: A new love and various other magickal uses, according to the bloom's color. A rose is often the central flower in a tussie-mussie.

SAGE: Sage stands for wisdom. Try using purple sages and tricolor sages for variety.

SWEET PEA: Symbolizes delicate pleasures. This flower is fragrant and very old-fashioned.

THYME: Use both the flowers and leaves for starting a new project.

VERONICA: Brings about a rapid recovery and continued vitality.

WILD STRAWBERRIES: Perfection—and you thought those wild strawberry "weeds" growing in your yard weren't good for anything! I've said it before, but it bears repeating: Magick *is* to be found all around you.

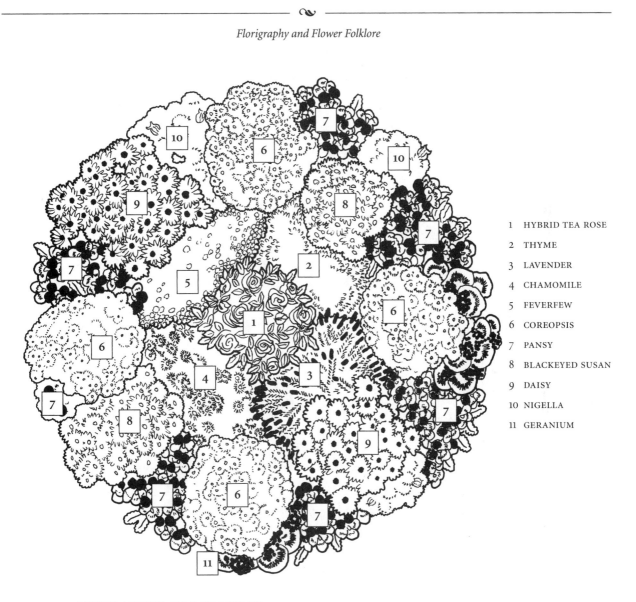

1   HYBRID TEA ROSE
2   THYME
3   LAVENDER
4   CHAMOMILE
5   FEVERFEW
6   COREOPSIS
7   PANSY
8   BLACKEYED SUSAN
9   DAISY
10 NIGELLA
11 GERANIUM

TUSSIE-MUSSIE GARDEN LAYOUT

How could such sweet and wholesome hours
be reckoned but in herbs and flowers?

ANDREW MARVELL

Enchanted Specialty Gardens

Specialty gardens, such as enchanted shade and moonlight gardens, are the focus of this chapter. We'll cover children's harvest gardens and container gardens as well. All of these plants or container combinations I have successfully grown myself. By no means are these the only plants you have available to you. Take these ideas and then make them your own. Feel free to try different variations—the sky is the limit! These are merely some plants that have grown well for me and will work in many gardens in the United States.

Shady Sorceress Gardens

If you have a vast amount of shade, don't fret. A shady magick garden can be a hauntingly beautiful place. I have gardens that surround my house—front, back, and side yards. However, the garden that gets the most compliments is the shade garden.

When you start a garden under older, established trees, you already have structure. Amending the soil with composted manure and peat moss is your first step. Shade plants require fertile soil, rich in organic matter. Keeping your plants watered in high summer and for the rest of the growing season is critical. You want moist soil, not soggy.

Mulch your plants, but no more than two inches deep. It helps retain moisture and, in time, as the mulch breaks down, it will add organic matter to your soil. Here are four words for you to live by: "Mulch is our friend."

Magickal herbs and plants that grow well in the part shade to full shade gardens are not difficult to find. Here is another witch's dozen of plants for you to try. As before, the common name is listed in bold print, followed by the botanical name in italics. These are followed by the plant's magickal correspondences and gardening growing tips.

A Witch's Dozen of Shady Plants

BLEEDING HEART (*Dicentra spectabilis*). Magickal uses include recovering from a broken heart and lost love. (Well, I mean *honestly*, were you expecting anything else?) Bleeding heart's pendant, heart-shaped flowers bloom in early spring. It grows about three feet tall. A cottage garden classic, bleeding heart is an excellent cut flower, and the foliage is attractive in the vase as well. Plants will die back to the ground in summer. Also available in a white variety. Zones 3–9.

COLUMBINE (*Aquilegia*). Utilized in spells for courage and love. Seeds were crushed and used to attract a mate. A favorite shady plant grown in the garden for centuries, these flowers reseed and grow two to three feet in height. Many colors are available (use different colors according to magickal need). Many hybrid columbines are hardy in zones 5–9.

FERNS. For faery magick and invisibility. Burn the dried fronds to attract rain. Many species are available. Check with other gardeners to see which variety grows well in your area. Ostrich fern (*Matteucia pensylvancia*) is usually a hardy, easy variety to try. They send out lots of babies after they are established. The ostrich fern is hardy in zones 2–8.

FORGET-ME-NOTS (*Myosotis*). Improves memory, and also may be used to help another remember you, i.e., a job interview or a new friend. Another shady plant that's admired by the faeries, it bears small clusters of blue flowers. Plants grow eight inches to two feet high, depending on the variety. A great plant for woodland gardens, there are new varieties that are available in pink as well. Forget-me-nots will grow in most zones—3–11.

FOXGLOVE (*Digitalis*). Magickally used for protection, and also a faery favorite, foxglove bears many folk names: fairy fingers, folk's gloves, witches' bells, and witches' thimbles, just to name a few. A great perennial species is yellow foxglove (*Digitalis grandiflora*), which grows to about two feet tall and blooms in late spring–early summer. It will sometimes rebloom if you dead-head it. Foxglove is toxic, and should not be ingested. Yellow foxglove is hardy from zones 4–9.

HOSTAS (*Hosta* species and cultivars). A leaf or two tucked into a vase full of other magickal flowers will add good luck and health. Hostas are a shade-loving perennial, also known as "Funkia." These old standards of the shade garden add mystery to your shade gardens and come in dozens of colors, from all shades of green, chartreuse, leaves with white stripes, and leaves that have contrasting edges. There is also a dusky blue-green variety. Choose your favorite—if you can. Height and leaf size depends on the variety. Plant height may range anywhere from one to four feet tall. The hosta produces pale purple flowers in midsummer. There are some new fragrant varieties available. Most varieties of hostas are hardy in zones 3–8.

IRIS. The three main petals of the flower stand for faith, knowledge, and bravery. The root is most often employed in magick. Orris root comes from the roots or rhizomes of the *Iris germanica* var. *florentina* iris plant. Orris root is used to draw love and as a fixative in potpourris and sachets (it helps to hold the scent). The iris is a popular spring bloomer, available in many colors. This is the sacred flower of Iris, the Greek goddess of the rainbow and messenger of the gods. The iris has been cultivated for centuries. There are two most common species of the iris: The Japanese iris is hardy to zones 5–10, and the Siberian iris is hardy from zones 4–9.

LADY'S MANTLE (*Alchemilla*). Love and attraction. Traditionally an alchemist's favorite, lady's mantle is a compact plant with round, fuzzy, gray-green leaves. A folk name is dewdrop, owing to the manner in which the plant's fluted leaves hold water droplets (they look like liquid silver on the leaves). In late spring or early summer, lady's mantle will bloom a spray of chartreuse green flowers. This perennial grows eighteen inches in height. It makes a pretty front-of-the-border plant. Zones 3–9.

MEADOWSWEET (*Filipendula ulmaria*). Love, weddings, and peace. Meadowsweet was a favorite fragrant herb in Elizabethan times. So often was it in demand for bridal flowers and weddings that it became known as bride-wort. Meadowsweet has creamy white flowers with an almond scent. It will bloom off and on during the summer. Grown best in partial shade, this hardy perennial can grow from two to four feet in height and prefers alkaline soils. Zones 4–7 or 8.

PANSIES (*Viola*). Sacred to Cupid, these bright, happy flowers are for easing an aching heart and lovesickness. Folk names include johnny jump-ups, heartsease, love-in-idleness, and kiss-me-at-the-garden-gate. Pansies may be grown as an annual or perennial. I use them in pots and containers in early spring. They will tolerate cold and even some snow. If planted in the garden in the fall and mulched with leaves, pansies will bloom even heavier again the following spring. Pansies thrive in partial or full shade. They do not tolerate hot summers.

SNAPDRAGONS (*Antirrhinum majus*). Protection and breaking hexes. Snapdragons are fun annuals to grow in your shade gardens, and in containers too! In Missouri, we have very intense, hot summers with high humidity; snaps planted with a full sun exposure in my garden tend to get a little toasty, but they thrive in part shade.

The elemental correspondence for snapdragons is fire. A faery plant that is popular with children, snaps are available in many colors and sizes. They also make an excellent cut flower. If your winter season is mild, they may survive the cold or reseed themselves for the next season.

SOLOMON'S SEAL (*Polygonatum*). The root is employed in protection and exorcism rituals. Adding a few blooms to a vase of flowers may be used to fight off negativity. A woodland plant and a wildflower native to the eastern United States, the lightly scented flowers bloom in late spring. There are several species, including a variegated variety. Zones 5–9.

TOUCH-ME-NOT (*Impatiens*). To be magickally used when time is of the essence. Another folk name is "Busy Lizzy." The most popular annual shade bedding plant, impatiens come in a wide variety of colors and patterns. Easy to grow and free blooming, they are a great border plant for adding seasonal color to shade gardens. Impatiens are annuals and will not survive a frost or any cold temperatures. Try white and pastel-colored impatiens for moonlight gardens.

Types of Shade and Plant Suggestions

Types of shade will vary from garden to garden. Understanding what type of shade you are working with will make it easier for you to achieve success in the garden. There are varying degrees of shade: partial shade (sometimes called dappled), medium shade, and full shade.

PARTIAL SHADE is to be found in areas that receive three to six hours of sunlight per day, or dappled sunlight all day. This dappled type of shade is usually found under the canopies of younger trees or older trees with a higher, more open canopy. Try these magickal flowering herbs: angelica, betony, catmint, coneflowers, obedient plant (*Physostegia virginiana*), foxglove, heliotrope, iris, lady's mantle, lilies, mallows, meadowsweet, mints, and soapwort.

MEDIUM SHADE can be classified as an area that is shady during the brightest hours of the day (the hours from 10:00 A.M. to 4:00 P.M.). This type of garden will catch some early morning rays if it faces the east or, conversely, late evening sun if the garden faces the west. Try these mystical plants and shrubs: astilbe, bleeding heart, coleus, ferns, forget-me-nots, hosta, monarda, impatiens, lobelia, lungwort (*Pulmonaria* species), and European wild ginger. Try planting these shrubs at the back of your shade garden for structure:
oak leaf hydrangea, big leaf hydrangeas, and viburnum.

FULL SHADE exists beneath the canopies of mature trees that have thick foliage, or in areas where shadows are cast by a neighboring house or garden structure, such as a shed or a privacy fence. These gardens may receive only a few hours of sunlight per day. These plants should perform well for you: bugleweed (*Ajuga*), columbine, dead nettle, ferns, ivy, lily of the valley, mints, Solomon's seal, tansy, and the violet.

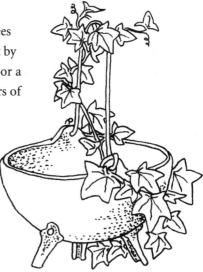

A black cat among roses,
phlox, lilac-misted under a quarter moon,
the sweet smells of heliotrope and night-
scented stock. The garden is very still.
It is dazed with moonlight,
contented with perfume . . .

AMY LOWELL, *THE GARDEN BY MOONLIGHT*

Flowers and Foliage for Moonlight Gardens

There is something entrancing about a moonlight garden. Moonlight gardens are all about fragrance, subtle color, and atmosphere, with the emphasis placed on flowers that release their perfumes after sundown. Fragrance is often our most powerful memory trigger. I still associate lilacs with my Grandma Doris. She had huge lilac shrubs growing alongside her house in the city. When I was a child, my sister and I used to play underneath and inside of them—it was like being inside a fragrant, purple cave.

Color is an all-important aspect of moonlight gardens. Pastel colors, silvery or pale green foliage, and as many white blooming plants as you can find will perform their own magick at twilight. Flower colors that really pop at night include white, cream, yellow, and pale pink. If you want to try your hand at moonlight gardens, look for those colors in bedding plants this year. You can add some of these colors to the perennial garden layout on page 78.

If you have sunny gardens and would like to try growing a moonlight garden, try these annual plants: geraniums, cleome, allysum, stock, cosmos, and white and yellow zinnias. Just to make things interesting, try adding dark purple petunias—not for their color, for their fragrance. You won't be able to see those velvety-looking purple blooms at night, but trust me, you won't have to. The fragrance they pump out after sundown will lead you right to them every time. Want to try a fragrant blooming shrub? The white variety of the lilac is another

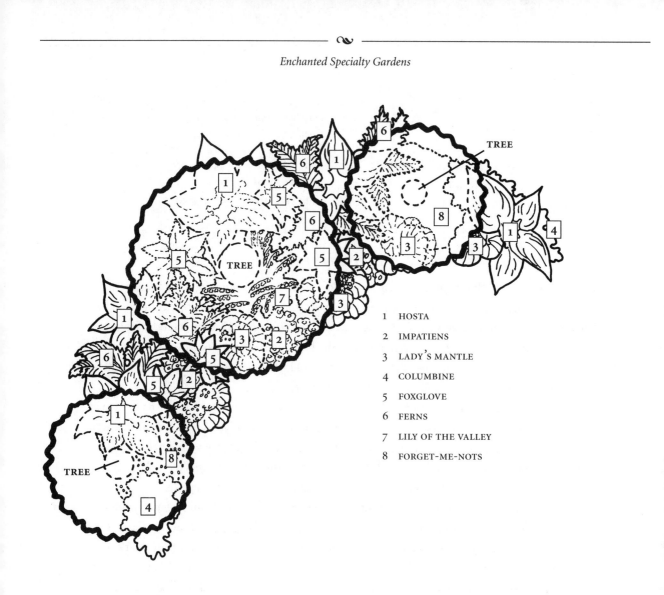

1   HOSTA

2   IMPATIENS

3   LADY'S MANTLE

4   COLUMBINE

5   FOXGLOVE

6   FERNS

7   LILY OF THE VALLEY

8   FORGET-ME-NOTS

SHADY OR MOONLIGHT GARDEN LAYOUT

sunny garden option. Here is a tip: All varieties of blooming plants that are white will have the term *alba* behind the name.

For a night-fragrant blooming bulb, try the perfumed fairy lilies (*Chlidanthus fragrans*) and Madonna lilies (*Lilium candidum*). The Madonna lily is an excellent magickal plant, with the attributes of protection and breaking love spells. The flower is also sacred to the Lady.

For an easy to grow perennial, try other varieties of daylilies (*Hemerocallis*). Hit the nursery early in the season, before Mother's Day, for the best selection. Many daylilies are fragrant, and the paler the color, the more they will stand out in your moonlight garden. Look for these varieties: Green Ice, a pale yellow flower with a green throat; Fairy Tale Pink, a pink flower with a pale green throat; Happy Treasure, a yellow and rose-pink mixture, and Java Sea, a neon-yellow bloom with an acid-green throat. For the magickal associations, match up the colors of the blooms with your Flower Color Magick Chart, found on pages 38.

Nicotiana (pronounced *niko-SHEE-anna*), the flowering tobacco, has a pale green variety that is very aromatic at night. These star-shaped annuals are another beloved flower that I add to my gardens every year. Nicotiana will last until frost and requires only occasional dead-heading to keep them blooming at their peak all summer long. If the flower production fades, cut them back to the leaves and they will shoot up again and bloom with more vigor. Also available in reds and pinks, try to get as many of the white and pale green as you can find. Your nose will be glad that you did. Nicotiana's magickal qualities are healing and purification.

Pale climbing roses, such as New Dawn, are a bewitching choice to climb over an arbor. A lovely ivory-pink color, climbing New Dawn is rated one of the best climbers for the Midwest region. Other climbing vines include the white clematis, wisteria, honeysuckle, and night-blooming jasmine. Any of these would be gorgeous alternatives.

It is with flowers as with moral qualities;
the bright are sometimes poisonous,
but I believe never the sweet.

PARK BENJAMIN, AMERICAN EDITOR
(1809-1864)

Shady Characters and Poisonous Plants

Some of my favorite cottage garden plants for the moonlight/shade garden are, unfortunately, poisonous: lily of the valley, moonflower vine (*Impomea alba*), and white and yellow foxgloves. I bided my time and waited until my kids were older before I planted these. You may want to do the same. There is a list of poisonous plants at the end of this section.

The first year we grew moonflower vines in the garden, all of the neighborhood kids started hanging out in the backyard to watch the moonflowers bloom. Every night at dusk the kids would show up to watch them open. Some evenings it would be just my family on the back patio enjoying the show. Other nights we had anywhere from six to a dozen kids and their assorted lawn chairs spread out across the garden. (And yes, the kids were supervised.) I even had a neighbor videotape the six-inch blooms as they shuddered open one evening.

As the moonflowers start to unfurl, they tremble and quiver. Before your eyes they slowly open up, like in a time-lapse special effect. The scent is haunting and downright enchanting. On an interesting note, moonflowers will attract both hawk moths and luna moths to your garden.

Moonflower vines are something that we continue to grow every year. (As I have no toddlers running amok through the garden, the moonflowers are safe enough for growing up the privacy fence.) If one of my young nieces or nephews should arrive, they are never left unsupervised in the garden anyway.

Another fascinating plant is the datura or angel's trumpet (*Datura inoxia* subspecies). This is a gothic witch garden plant, with a capitol *G* for gothic and grim. It is an absolutely extraordinary night-scented flower, but I want to warn you to *be careful* with this plant! They are incredibly poisonous.

As a young gardener who didn't know any better, I once bought a home-grown shade plant from a vender at a flea market. He had photographs of it in bloom and he told me that the plant was called a "moonflower bush." Captivated with my find, I planted it in my shade garden, fertilized it, and watched. As the summer progressed, it started to form huge trumpet-shaped buds.

The first time that it bloomed was on the night of a full moon. Excited by the timing, I checked on it periodically throughout the evening to discover that the flower had an amazingly heady, musky-lemony fragrance. It was so strong that it made my stomach turn over, and it immediately made me suspicious. I sat down in the garden and had a little chat with this two-foot plant. My shade gardens are behind a privacy fence and under old maple trees, so I settled there under the full moon, alone and unobserved.

I closed my eyes and held my hands out over the blooms and asked (in my mind) for the plant to tell me who it really was. The answer that came into my mind was just one word . . . *death*. I fell over backward in my haste to get away from the plant and scooted away from a safe distance of three feet to stare at it.

"Okay," I said to myself, as my heart pounded hard in my throat, "that was different."

I had never had anything like that happen to me before. I wanted another opinion. So, after a few moments, I called all the kids outside and showed them the plant. I told them nothing of my "discovery" and asked them what they thought about it. My kids are usually a fool-proof barometer if something is wrong, whether it's people or situations. To my consternation all three of them frowned and two of the three made no move to touch it. My second son started to reach out and then yanked his hand away at the last moment. (He's the one with the most pronounced psychic abilities, I might add.) They all told me immediately that they didn't like it. Since the children were young at that time, I warned all three of them to stay away from it until I could correctly identify this "moonflower bush." I then herded every-one inside to wash their hands, just in case.

The next day I headed to the library and hit the books. To my dismay I discovered that my moonflower bush was actually a datura. All parts of this plant—flowers, leaves, and seed pods—are extremely toxic. It was even in capital bold-faced letters in all the books: ALL PARTS OF THIS PLANT ARE DEADLY. Damn. Well, I learned my lesson. So much for buy-ing unmarked flowers. It was a lovely plant and I didn't want to just kill it. I kept the kids away from it and then when it started to fade and set seed pods, I used surgical gloves and ripped the plant out and disposed of it inside of a few garbage bags. I had my husband care-fully apply a weed killer on the area, just in case I missed anything.

The other perennials eventually crept back in but, to this day, nothing will grow in the original spot where the datura was planted. After a while I planted an oak leaf hydrangea shrub (*Hydrangea quercifolia*) in the area. Its off-white, cone-shaped blooms are an accent to the shade/moonlight garden, as are its orange leaves in the fall. One of my favorite blooming shrubs, this hydrangea has grown well and it now covers up the bare spot. Magickally, you may use the bark of hydrangeas to ward off negativity and for hex breaking.

For more shady/moonlight garden perennials, try campanula, pale yellow daffodils, snowy white tulips, snowdrops, spiderwort, the pearly astilbe Snowdrift, and white phlox. Some other varieties of herbs that will thrive in shade are angelica, which will grow best for you in part shade, as will mallows and catnip. As mentioned before, pastel impatiens and white begonias are charming additions, as they will stand out well at night in a shady bed. Sil-ver lamb's ears and the white-edged hosta are also good choices. Chartreuse shades of the hosta are an option for foliage that will glow after sundown. Finally, to accent your moonlight garden, string up a strand of white lights to add a magickal sparkle.

Poisonous Garden Plants

By no means is this list all inclusive, it is only meant to be informative. There are many other poisonous plants that are not represented here. If you are interested in pursuing this topic further, check with your local botanical garden or call your county's Master Gardeners for more information. Also, there are several excellent "Poisonous Plants" websites available to you on the Internet. Some of the best are from Cornell University, North Carolina State University, and Pennsylvania University.

If situations occur where poisoning concerns exist, then I recommend contacting a poison control hotline right away. The National Poison Control Hotline (for adults and children) is 1-800-222-1222. This number will connect you to your local hotlines. The National Animal Poison Control Center's number is 1-888-426-4435.

Please note the * denotes popular landscaping shrubs that are toxic when eaten in large quantities.

Amaryllis	Bouncing bet (seeds are toxic)
American holly	Burning bush *
Azaleas	Caladium
Angel's trumpet (*Datura*)	Chinese lantern
Baby's breath	Clematis
Baneberry	Coleus
Belladonna	Crocus (all parts)
Blackberry lily	Daffodils
Bleeding heart	Daphne (berries are toxic)
Bittersweet	Datura

Delphinium, a.k.a. larkspur

Dock

Dutchman's breeches

Flax

Four o'clock

Foxglove

Helleborus

Niger

Hyacinth

Hydrangea *

Great lobelia, cardinal flower

Iris (rhizomes)

Jack-in-the-pulpit

Japanese honeysuckle (berries)

Lantana

Lily of the valley

Lobelia

Monkshood (*Aconite*),
    a.k.a. wolf's bane

Moonflower (mildly toxic)

Morning glories (mildly toxic)

Oak leaf hydrangea *

Oleander

Peace lily

Plumbago

Poinsettia

Pokeweed (all parts)

Poppies

Rhubarb (the leaves)

Rue

Stonecrop (Sedum)

Snow-on-the-mountain

Sorrel

Star of Bethlehem
    (*Orithogalum umbellatum*)

Sweet pea

Tobacco

Tomato (foliage)

Trumpet creeper

Virginia creeper (highly toxic)

White snakeroot

Windflower

Wisteria

Yew

Samhain/Harvest Pumpkin Garden

Here are some tips and tricks that I have learned over the years while growing pumpkins, gourds, and Indian corn. My husband, kids, and I have been raising pumpkins and fall ornamentals for years. We select the ones we want for ourselves and then we invite all of our nieces and nephews over (at last count there were fifteen of them) to choose their pumpkins. My sisters-in-law pick from the gourds, mini pumpkins, and corn to decorate their homes. See a sample garden layout on page 88.

In late September, my kids set up a little pumpkin stand in the front yard and then sell their harvest to the neighborhood families for Halloween. We don't make a huge amount of money, they do it for fun. I split the profit in half, and divide it between the three of them and let them spend the first half however they want. The other half of the money is put away for Yule, for their gift exchange with each other.

Growing

First things first. You need a lot of space to grow pumpkins. If you are limited to a small backyard vegetable garden, try the mini varieties such as Baby Boo or Jack Be Little. Pumpkins require very fertile, rich soil. We grow our pumpkins down at the family farm. The soil at the farm is incredibly black and rich, as it's flood-plain soil. However, we still make our hills for the pumpkins with bags of composted manure—not raw manure, the composted kind that you buy in twenty-five pound bags at the garden center.

For my part of the country, farmers recommend having your pumpkins and gourds planted by June 7. I live in zone 5. Check with the local farmers or your county's extension office to see what planting time they recommend.

For directions in planting Indian or ornamental corn, check the seed packet for variety-specific planting dates, which are usually after the last frost date, when the soil temperature is warm, at least sixty-five degrees. Plant in side-by-side rows for pollination purposes, and try a nitrogen-rich fertilizer for the corn.

Stake your pumpkin hills with a tall stake when you plant the seeds. Pumpkin foliage grows anywhere from one foot to three feet tall, and then you can't find the hills to water them. (Learned that lesson the hard way, myself.) Don't step on the vines! Fertilize your pumpkins regularly with a water-soluble fertilizer like Miracle-gro.

Watch for signs of squash beetle activity and be prepared to dust the pumpkins. I recommend Sevin, or Bug Be Gone. It's an all-purpose powdered pesticide that kills those bugs. Sevin is a fairly safe chemical to apply topically to pumpkins and other vegetables. It is not absorbed into the plant, and washes off easily (the residual life of Sevin is fairly short). Dust safely! Wear a mask and gloves. The first time I grew pumpkins I announced that we would not use any chemicals. We had a beauty of a crop that year, too, hundreds of them. Then the squash beetles found us. They attach themselves to the vines and drain all the juice out of the pumpkins, so they look like deflated playground balls. The attack of the vampire pumpkin bugs! Nasty. We lost the entire patch that year, and I changed my mind about chemicals.

To discourage squash beetles, you can try planting marigolds, catnip, tansy, and nasturtiums. Also, when choosing your varieties for pumpkins, look for mildew-resistant varieties. A problem with mildew widely affected the pumpkin crops in Missouri last year. It's just one of those things. For the first time in years, we had to buy pumpkins for Samhain. We lost our whole patch.

Harvesting

By late July or early August, the Indian corn should be mature. After gathering them, gently peel back the husks. String up some rope to hang the ears on and let the corn dry out completely. Use a protected area, like your garage or a shed. If you leave them outside the birds will get them.

In mid to late September, watch your foliage on the pumpkin and gourd vines. I know the pumpkins are starting to turn orange, but sit tight. Wait until the foliage dies back and the stems start to turn brown before you harvest them. Use a sharp pocket knife to cut the vines, remembering to leave yourself a good stem length.

Carry pumpkins like a ball, not by the stem. Wash them in a solution of bleach and water when you get them home. The bleach water helps stop mildew and washes off any chemical residue. Store your pumpkins and gourds on wood planks or hay bales, not on concrete (they'll rot).

Selling

Open your yard stand in late September–early October. Let the kids do the selling. Just keep them supervised. Once a stretch limo pulled up in front of our house and the chauffeur, in uniform, hopped out to buy some pumpkins for his kids. He scared the hell out of my youngest son and daughter, who were about seven and eight years old at the time. (They thought the limo was a hearse.) Once I explained to them that he was driving a bride and groom around in there, not a dead body, they thought that was kind of cool.

I watch my kids through the front window, even now. If there is a problem I just step up to the door or walk out onto the front porch. Usually it's just someone who wants to know where we grew the pumpkins, or needs to break a large bill. Have change available.

Let your kids make up a few signs. People love to buy from children. Toss gourds into a wheelbarrow and let people root around through them. They enjoy doing it and I've yet to

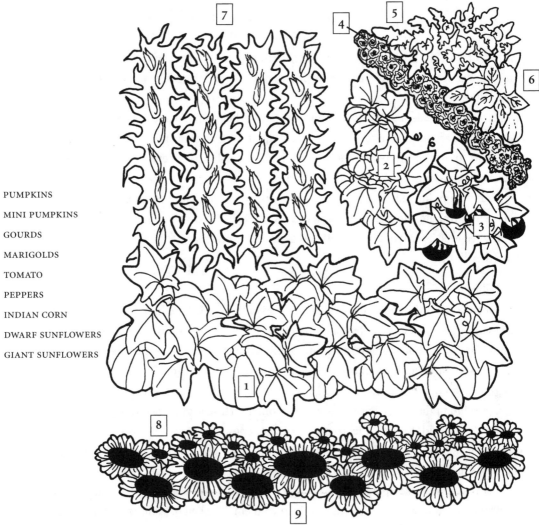

1   PUMPKINS

2   MINI PUMPKINS

3   GOURDS

4   MARIGOLDS

5   TOMATO

6   PEPPERS

7   INDIAN CORN

8   DWARF SUNFLOWERS

9   GIANT SUNFLOWERS

CHILDREN'S HARVEST GARDEN LAYOUT

figure out why. Also the wheelbarrow is handy; when you're done for the day, just roll the wheelbarrow around back.

Display Indian corn or really pretty mini pumpkins on a card table. Ornamental corn is fragile when it dries, so don't be too rough on the husks.

Don't haggle over prices, clearly mark on the pumpkins close to the stem with a ball-point pen. Make your prices very reasonable, price them to move. You don't want to get stuck with thirty extra pumpkins, do you? Either give away any extras that are left over, donate them to a shelter for troubled kids, carve them up for a large Halloween display, or use them as compost.

> *But a little garden, the littler the better, is your*
> *richest chance of happiness and success.*
>
> REGINALD FARRER

Bewitching Container Gardens

Container gardening is at an all-time level of popularity. If you are limited in space, this may be your only option. You can create a fabulous garden simply with containers, window boxes, and hanging baskets in all different shapes and sizes. Turn your patio, balcony, or deck into a miniature garden that is easy to move around or rearrange.

Remember, you're not limited to flowers. There is more to container gardens than just annuals. You can grow herbs and vegetables, such as tomatoes and peppers. Strawberries can be successfully grown in hanging baskets. Lettuce may be grown in containers; I have even seen a shorter variety of carrots grown in large pots.

In the past when I have taught the public how to make their own container gardens, I gave them several themes to choose from. So I'll do the same for you as well. Of the many different combinations of plants that I have suggested, I also included some popular cooking herbs.

Experiment with these suggestions. When you plant your flower containers, plant them full. You will be dead-heading these as the season progresses. You want those pots to look full when you start. It's depressing to see a half-filled container because you're waiting for the plants to get larger. Remember to fertilize your containers every two weeks, and water them every day.

To maintain vigorous plant growth and to keep your plants attractive, remove spent, dried-up flowers and seed pods. By removing these, the plant puts its energies into producing more flowers, as opposed to putting its energies into seed production. To prune, follow the stem down to the first leaf junction and clip the stem there.

Kitchen Witch Container Garden

In a large pot, try planting together rosemary, parsley, sage, chives, bouquet dill, garlic, and basil. These practical seasonings and cooking herbs (that's what I tell the general public anyway) are very easy to grow together in a sunny location. To my witch friends, I pass along these magickal correspondences. In order, they include love and healing from the rosemary; protection and purification from the parsley; wisdom from sage; chives are great for absorbing negativity; we get protection again from the dill; garlic is worked into exorcism rituals; and the basil gives us wealth and good luck. Now that is a handy little combination to have around, don't you think?

Fragrant Container Garden

For a fabulous mixture of textures and scents, try an arrangement of any of the following fragrant plants: miniature roses, catnip, lavender, mint, or scented geraniums. Plant these in a large pot and place in a sunny location. If you want the roses to survive the winter, transplant them into your garden to winter over. Magickal uses are as follows: roses for love and, depending on the color, other applications (see pages 11 and 38); mint bestows prosperity; catnip is for, oddly enough, cat magick; and scented geraniums are protective.

Veggie Combos

For vegetable container gardening, go with a classic: a patio tomato variety and marigolds. Planting marigolds and tomatoes together are beneficial, and is called companion planting. Marigolds prevent bugs from infesting the tomatoes, and the plants are usually stronger and more disease resistant as well. Cherry tomatoes are a fun variety for children to try, as are green peppers and marigolds. Make sure that you give them lots of sun, fertilizer, and water. This planter would work well for growing on your deck or balcony. The magickal correspondence for tomatoes is love; in fact, an old folk name for the tomato was the "love apple."

Also, according to *Cunningham's Encyclopedia of Magical Herbs*, "when a tomato is placed on the window sill or any other household entrance, it repels evil from entering." Hmm . . . good to know.

> *Would that this garland fair*
> *Might weave around thy life*
> *A spell to shield from care*
> *A guard from every strife.*
>
> ANONYMOUS

House-Warding Plant Combinations

To ward your home and property is like placing a permanent protective psychic shield against outside influences around your house and yard. Our homes naturally exude a shield of energy. Usually witches and other magick users deliberately strengthen theirs. How? They grow plants with protective properties around the house, place crystals inside the home, display hex signs on the outside of the house, or often hang a horseshoe, open end up, over the inside front door.

Garden witch containers for protection are a subtle type of magick. It's not expensive or hard to do. Start with some good potting mix and your container of choice, and add a little garden witch flair.

Pagan Family Protection Combo

For a part sun–afternoon shade spot, plant trailing ivy, snapdragons, allysum, pink geraniums, and dark purple petunias in a hanging basket or container by your front door. Why these plants? Ivy is protective; snaps ward off negative spells; allysum expels charms; pink geraniums are for love; and dark purple petunias add power and are very fragrant at night.

Hot Spot Container

For a very hot and sunny location, this plant combo will hold up to intense summer heat and then last into the fall. Group together zinnias, coxcomb, and marigolds in a container of your choosing. Zinnias are pretty annuals that make great cut flowers for the vase, come in an array of hot colors, and attract butterflies as well. The red coxcomb is protective and aids in healing. Marigolds have the astrological correspondence of the sun; this flower is used to repel evil and nightmares. It features prominently in the Mexican festival El Dia de los Muertos, the day of the dead. This celebration begins at midnight on November 1, and is a national holiday in Mexico that honors the spirits of deceased ancestors and loved ones.

White Witch Window Box

Red geraniums for protection and to guard the home; vinca vine for its many magickal properties that I listed before—okay, okay, I'll list them again: bindings, protection, love, and prosperity. Allysum for fragrance and to break manipulative spells, and blue lobelia to halt gossip. This container will tolerate part sun/part shade. Be advised that the lobelia will wither back in intense summer heat, but when it cools off again it should bloom back out.

White Witch Combo for the Shade

Instead of geraniums, plant shade-loving double begonias in the window box. Double begonias resemble a rose in full bloom. They have heavy, waxy petals, and are available in many colors, such as reds, pinks, orange-coral shades, and yellow. Use the color correspondence chart from chapter 3 to match the color to your intent. Use the vinca vine, blue lobelia, and white or purple allysum to fill out your boxes.

The last two combinations are inspired by a lady that I met years ago at the very first nursery job that I ever had, which taught me many invaluable lessons. But by far the most memorable experience was the day an elderly lady came strolling into the nursery, demanding some assistance in choosing flowers for her window boxes. All the other staff took one look at her and scattered. She seemed harmless enough to me, leaning on her cane and grinning at me.

As I walked around the nursery with her and helped her choose her flowers, she told me little tidbits of plant lore that I had never heard of before. She pointed, I fetched and carried. It was an interesting half hour. I thought I was being very discreet. I made sure I said "folklore" when I asked a question, or I said something like, "What's the story of this one?" There was no talk of magick.

Later, when I was able to double-check on those meanings of all the flowers that she had told me about, they matched up. Every one of them.

We ended up going with one of my favorite window box combinations, the one listed previously—red geraniums, vinca vines, blue lobelia, and white allysum. As I helped her load her purchases in the back of an old station wagon, she turned to me and said, "When I was a girl, my grandmother always told me that you could spot the good witches in the neighborhood by the red geraniums in their window boxes."

I almost dropped the flats of flowers, I was so surprised by her comment. She just smiled blandly and continued by telling me, "Another way to tell was to look and see if they planted red geraniums or red begonias in circles around their trees." She cackled at my startled expression, patted me on the arm, and started for the driver's side of her car. So much for being discreet. She tossed her cane in, turned back to look at me, and asked, "What color of geraniums do you have in your boxes at home, girl?"

"Red ones," I told her honestly.

"I thought so." She laughed, climbed into her old car, and gunned it out of the parking lot. I never saw her again, but I have never forgotten her.

So wherever you are, Ma'am, thanks . . . and blessed be.

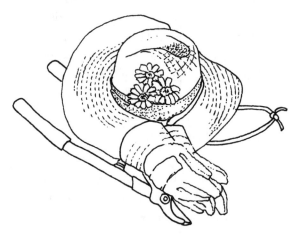

6

My roses are my jewels, the sun and moon my
clocks, fruit and water my food and drink.

HESTER LUCY STANHOPE

ᏣᏊ

Moon Gardening, Magick, and Astrological Timing

A natural way to reap the benefits of astrological timing is to plant and harvest with the phases of the moon. This gives your garden witchery a big magickal boost. Gardening in harmony with the waxing and waning of the moon is a tradition that spans many, many years.

I was first introduced to the rudiments of moon gardening as a young bride by my husband's grandmother. At the family's farm, Grandma was always very insistent about when the potatoes were planted. She said we should plant as close to St. Patrick's Day as we could get and be in the proper phase of the moon. It was how they had always done things.

This made me curious, so I asked her about it. Her response was that was the way her folks had planted, and all the "old timers" planted that way. Gardening with the phases of the moon . . . sounded kind of witchy to me. I was intrigued.

If you mention moon gardening to most horticulturists, they get a little bent out of shape. I had a college professor sneeringly inform my horticulture class that moon gardening was just a faery tale. This comment was made by the same person who thought it was riveting to look at a two-hour slide presentation of his compost piles.

Moon gardening is a fascinating way to add a little of that old-time magick into your gardening. Try it for yourself and see what kinds of results you get.

The Moon was but a Chin of Gold
a night or two ago—
And now She turns Her perfect Face
Upon the World below—

EMILY DICKINSON

Easy Moon Gardening

New Moon to First Quarter Moon

This first quarter moon phase occurs between the new moon and the seven days following. This moon rises in the morning and the crescent moon is seen as a thin curve in the western sky after sunset. Each night, the moon gains dimension and appears higher in the western sky, as the moon moves farther along into the phase.

Plant above-ground crops such as lettuce, spinach, cucumbers, corn, onions, and spinach. Plant flowering annuals like impatiens, petunias, geraniums, and annual flowering herbs. Sow seeds and transplant. Prune now to encourage more growth.

Second Quarter to Full Moon

This moon phase begins approximately seven days after the new moon. Do you need an easy way to tell for sure if the moon is in the second quarter phase? The moon will appear about half-full in the sky. This moon rises around noon and sets in the early hours of the morning.

Plant above-ground crops such as beans, squash, tomatoes, peppers, pumpkins, and watermelon. Continue to plant annual flowers during this waxing, second quarter moon phase.

Full Moon

The full moon rises at sundown and sets at daybreak. This moon phase begins approximately fourteen days after the new moon. The full moon is a time of increased power and a time for blessings. Try planting a favorite magickal herb now. Gather your magickal herbs and plants as the full moon rises and take advantage of the extra mystic energy that the full moon lends to them. Harvest fruits and veggies just after the full moon for increased flavor.

Third Quarter or Waning Moon

As the moon begins to move out of the full moon phase and into the third quarter, you will observe that the moon rises later and later in the evenings. It will appear to slowly lose its fullness from the right side. This seven-day time period is called the waning moon. This is the best time to plant perennials and trees.

Plant root vegetable crops such as potatoes, turnips, radishes, and carrots. Plant bulbs, biennials, and perennials. Plant trees and shrubs in the cool evening hours now. They will suffer less transplant shock in this waning moon phase, and water or rain is thought to run straight to the roots of the plants during this time.

Fourth Quarter to Dark Moon

The fourth quarter moon begins approximately seven days after the full moon. During the fourth quarter moon phase, the moon rises around two to three o'clock in the morning and sets during the afternoon. Do not plant; instead, till, cultivate, control weeds, and harvest. Lay out a plan for a new garden. Prune now to control growth.

> *The moon like a flower*
> *In heaven's high bower,*
> *With silent delight*
> *Sits and smiles on the night.*
>
> WILLIAM BLAKE

Moon Signs Are for Specializing

Being aware of the signs of the moon and their effects on spellwork is an important aspect of magick for garden witches. Just as the various moon signs influence our magick, so too does the moon influence the garden as it moves through the different zodiac signs.

All of the moon's zodiac signs will appear at least once a month and last for a two- to three-day time period. To discover what moon sign you are currently in, consult an up-to-date almanac, astrological calendar, or Llewellyn's annual *Moon Sign Book*.

Each separate moon sign has its own use for a specific gardening task. These tasks will be influenced by the element delegated to each moon sign.

FIRE DAYS are Aries, Leo, and Sagittarius. These days are for planning, designing new gardens, and maintenance. That means get in there and pull those weeds!

EARTH DAYS are Taurus, Virgo, and Capricorn. These earthy days are for the "dirty work" of gardening—shoveling, hoeing, thinning, and transplanting.

AIR DAYS are Gemini, Libra, and Aquarius. Use these days for communicating with the flower faeries and tree spirits. During the air sign days, plant your flowers, be they annual or perennial, sow seeds, and secure any climbing vines or roses.

WATER DAYS are Pisces, Cancer, and Scorpio. These days are for the irrigation and watering of your garden. Water the garden thoroughly.

So what's all the fuss about fire days as opposed to earth days, you may be wondering? It is a good way to specialize your magickal gardening. If you cannot catch the correct moon phase for your planting and harvesting, try working with the various moon signs instead. Or you may combine *both* the moon phase and the complementary moon sign for a one-two punch.

Imagine that you decide to buy a clematis for your garden. You snagged one on sale and take your treasure home to scout out a likely spot for your new flowering vine—somewhere where the base and the lower part of the plant will have shade, and the vine can grow to the sun.

As clematis vines can be finicky creatures and often take a few years to become established, you decide to stack the odds in your favor with a little magickal moon gardening. The best time for planting this perennial would be during a waning moon, on a Virgo moon sign day. Well, nuts. The moon phase happens to be waxing and the moon sign is in Leo. Now what do you do? Why, I thought you'd never ask.

You would check out the list below and notice that Virgo days are listed as good times for planting flowering vines. That would work out nicely. So if you can't catch the appropriate moon phase, a Virgo moon day would be another opportune time for planting your clematis.

Be patient for a few days. Set that clematis container in the shade, so it won't get roasted. (Nursery container plants can dry out quickly in full sun.) Give it a little dose of fertilizer now, and then water it well every day. Sit tight and when the moon sign hits Virgo, drag out your shovel and tuck that clematis into your garden.

MOON SIGNS FOR GARDENING

ARIES: Fire day; harvest, weed, or cultivate

TAURUS: Earth day; promotes robust growth

GEMINI: Air day; a favorable sign for harvesting and pulling weeds

CANCER: Water day; opportune for planting and transplanting

LEO: Fire day; great for harvesting scented herbs

VIRGO: Earth day, plant flowering vines now, as this encourages blooms, but little fruit

LIBRA: Air day; the flower sign

SCORPIO: Water day; good sign for planting shrubs and trees

SAGITTARIUS: Fire day; cultivate and pull weeds, or plan a new flower bed

CAPRICORN: Earth day; plant and transplant, the next best sign after Cancer

AQUARIUS: Air day; good for cultivation

PISCES: Water day; planting and watering

I am sure that you noticed other opportune times for flower planting when you went over the list, such as Taurus, Cancer, and Libra. Check the list again. Did you notice any more? How about Capricorn and Pisces? See, it's not hard. If you were really impatient and didn't want to wait, any of those signs would have worked for our imaginary clematis too. However, the Virgo day would have been your best shot.

I can tell you from personal experience that I usually have better luck with plants and vegetables if they are planted in the correct phase and/or sign of the moon. If I stumble across annual bedding plants (like impatiens) that are reduced to a really good price, I'll purchase them regardless of the moon phase. When I plant those sale impatiens to add color to the shade garden, I will instead try and catch a favorable moon sign for planting, if the moon phase is wrong.

Notice I said "try." Over the years I have seen the difference planting in the correct moon sign or phase can make. One summer I had guests coming over to specifically see the gardens, and my shade garden was sulking for some reason. In a panic, I ran out and bought some more impatiens for color and tucked them in. Did I check my moon phase or sign? Nope. (Give me a garden witch demerit.)

After a few weeks, my husband and I noticed that our new impatiens were not growing as well. We dosed them with fertilizer and waited. By the end of the season, the plants that were planted in the correct moon phase were noticeably taller and more robust. The ones I planted in a rush were healthy, but shorter and not blooming as nicely as their "correctly" planted neighbors. It made a believer out of me. My family thought my being impatient with impatiens was pretty funny. I took a lot of razzing about it until the frost nailed them all in the fall.

> *Live in each season as it passes; breathe the air,*
> *drink the drink, taste the fruit, and resign*
> *yourself to the influences of the earth.*
>
> HENRY DAVID THOREAU

Four Full Moon Gardening Celebrations

Speaking of the influences of the earth and the changing seasons, how about creating a ritual to correspond with the full moon closest to each solstice and equinox? Observing the various changing seasons at the full moon is a fantastic way to tune yourself in to the growth tides of the garden and the bounty of the earth.

The full moon closest to the vernal equinox could be employed to celebrate growth, change, loving partners, fertility, and the fecundity of the earth and your own body. The full moon that falls around the summer solstice may be used for love, prosperity, energy, health, and happiness. The full moon nearest the autumnal equinox, the harvest moon, is a time for thanksgiving, happy homes, sharing, and family. The full moon neighboring the winter solstice is for birth, new beginnings, plans for new projects, rest, relaxation, and peace.

Here are some ideas to help get you started on creating your own rituals. You may use these to bless your garden and yourself or to help you harmonize with the changing tides of nature. I have included an invocation, candle colors, plant, herb, and deity correspondences. Break out a nice bottle of white wine or light fruit juice. Treat yourself to some sugar cookies from the bakery or make your own. A recipe for easy esbat (full moon) cookies is included at the end of this section.

Winter Full Moon

At the full moon closest to the winter solstice, you may care to bless your garden while it is at rest during this winter season. Call for blessings on your home and family and petition the God and Goddess for peace. Even though it may be too cold to go and dig around in the garden, you can still enjoy it anyway. If you live in a warmer climate and have year-round flowers and plant activity, consider yourself very fortunate. For those of us who do not, this is the time to notice that, although your garden may be sleeping, life goes on around you nonetheless.

For example, the evergreen and the holly are still luxuriously green. Pine cones adorn the various spruces and pines. The hawthorn and crab apple trees still hold their fruit. Sparkling red berries brighten up the female holly. The birds will make good use of these treats throughout the winter months. Go fill up your bird feeder and enjoy watching the birds. Make your yard a safe, happy haven for the birds during the winter months. These signs of nature are precious to us during this time. As garden witches and natural magicians, we should celebrate and enjoy nature during *all* of her seasons.

CANDLES: White, dark green, and red.

PLANTS AND FLOWERS: Pine cones, winter berries, red roses, holly, small pine branches, oak leaves, and acorns.

GODS AND GODDESSES: The Mother and the newborn Sun God, the Oak and Holly King.

ACTION: Light a ritual fire in the fireplace or decorate a table or shelf with a Yule log studded with candles.

TIMING: Moon directly overhead or midnight.

> *The great wheel of the year now turns back to the light,*
> *As we hail the coming victory of the Oak King this night.*
> *The Holly King will pass away to return on Midsummer's eve,*
> *We welcome rebirth and renewal, in Yuletide's season of peace.*

Spring Full Moon

Go outside, take a deep breath. Do you smell spring in the air yet? It's coming. Take a quick look in the garden. This is the time of the year I am often pawing around in my flower beds, searching for signs of the crocus and the tender shoots of the earliest bulbs. My triumphant cries of discovery have often caused concerned neighbors to come over to ask me if I had lost something (like my mind) as I dig around under the leaves, looking for the crocus.

Pull aside those fallen leaves, see anything yet? Check out the trees in your area. The buds are swelling and the witch hazels may already be in bloom. Does your heart good, doesn't it? How can people *not* get caught up in the rush and wonder of spring? All of those new possibilities and fresh beginnings.

Draw up a simple plan for a new flower or herb bed this year. Narrow down your choices for plants. Get your seed selections ready, it won't be long now. As you celebrate the full moon closest to the vernal equinox, you could bless your plans for a new garden. Enchant your seeds and rejoice in the fertility of the earth and the coming bounty of your garden.

CANDLES: White, pink, and green.

PLANT AND FLOWERS: Tulips, hyacinths, and daffodils.

GODS AND GODDESSES: Eostre and the God as a youth.

ACTION: Color eggs, buy seed packets, or create plans for your new garden.

TIMING: Moon rise.

> *I call the Goddess Eostre, lady of green growing things,*
> *I celebrate the earth's fertility, this burgeoning time of spring.*
> *May the God grant me growth, patience, and the power to be wise,*
> *As the slowly rising Storm Moon illuminates the eastern skies.*

Summer Full Moon

Ah, summer. The garden is glorious and the herbs and flowers are growing and blooming. What better time to celebrate the exuberant magick and wonder of nature and the garden? If you care to add a subtle magickal theme to the garden, try adding a Green Man mask. This would be the perfect sly and very magickal accessory. The popular image of the Green Man is easy to find in garden-type gift shops. A Green Man is often depicted as a man's smiling face covered in leaves and foliage. The Green Man symbolizes the blessings of the God and his protective presence on your property.

The full moon closest to the summer solstice is traditionally employed to celebrate and enjoy the mystery and romance of the garden . . . must be all the lightning bugs and the scent of roses in the evening air. As night falls, the lightning bugs make their annual appearance. Children run about the yard, chasing them down and hoping to catch one. If they are successful, they giggle as the bugs crawl across their hands and then gasp in wonder as they fly slowly away.

As we come closer to the longest day of the year and the point where the sun reaches its zenith, we should work for the gentle blessing of rain and the protection of the crops that the farmers have worked so diligently to grow. Make sure that you are watering your plants and new trees. As the hottest part of the year begins, water is crucial to the garden's survival. Give the plants a dose of fertilizer to encourage their growth. It is not enough merely to plant the herbs and flowers in the garden, you must care for them as well. Celebrate your health, happiness, and your ability to be free. Observe the night sky, and go chase a couple of lightning bugs, just for the fun of it. I won't tell a soul.

CANDLES: Blue, yellow, and gold.

PLANTS AND FLOWERS: Summer fruits like berries, roses, a few sprigs of holly, green oak leaves and flowering herbs from the garden.

GODS AND GODDESSES: The Green Man, the Holly and the Oak King, all mother goddesses.

RITUAL BONFIRE: Alas, city ordinances often prohibit bonfires without special permission. Safety is a main issue as well—you wouldn't want to accidentally set someone's yard on fire! If you have a permit or permission to light a bonfire, be smart and safe. Keep hoses nearby and water at the ready. If a large bonfire is not an option for you, instead try building a small balefire in a old-style barbeque pit, or light several candles and then place them together, inside of a large metal cauldron. *Ta-da!* Instant balefire.

TIMING: When the moon is directly overhead or midnight.

The noble Green Man has once again returned,
On this grand night the blessed bonfires will burn.
Bring us prosperity and health, Great Mother, we pray,
As we celebrate the shortest night and the longest day.

Autumn Full Moon

The harvest moon. Traditionally the harvest moon got its name from the farmers who appreciated the extra light and extra work time that it gave them for gathering their crops. Due to the angle of the earth at this time of year, the moon looks huge as it rises. Often it appears gold or even bright orange as it ascends into the eastern sky.

As our season of gardening begins to wind down, we are rewarded with the glory of the changing leaves and the blessing of the cool, crisp evening air. Clip some spicy mums from the garden and bring them inside to brighten up your table. Rake some leaves together and start a leaf fight with your spouse or the kids. Go and pick out some charming tulip or daffodil bulbs and plant them now, so you can enjoy them in the garden next spring. Remember, fall is for planting, too.

Choose a pretty young tree or shrub from the nursery and plant it into your yard. This is the perfect time of the year to plant trees and shrubs, as they get to settle into their new homes and drop their leaves naturally. The cooler fall air and rains help them suffer less transplant shock. The tree or shrub will go dormant and rest during winter. Come spring, they are adjusted to their new home and ready to grow.

The harvest moon could be used to bless those new trees and shrubs, to celebrate the family and your happy home, and it is the perfect time to be thankful for the bounty of your garden, whether it was flowers for the vase, herbs for spells and charms, or simply vegetables for the kitchen table.

CANDLES: Red, orange, yellow, and brown.

PLANTS AND FLOWERS: Mums, asters, morning glory. Apples and pumpkins, grapes and grapevines. Oak leaves, acorns, and other turning leaves. Various herbs to match your magickal intent.

GODS AND GODDESSES: The Crone, Demeter, Persephone, and Hecate. The god of the vine, Dionysus.

TIMING: Sunset/moon rise.

Great Goddess, as your golden moon rises, we hail this season of plenty.
The garden's final bounty is gathered in, as the leaves turn colors gently.
There is a bite in the air as autumn, the season of the witch, sweeps in.
Let our days of thanksgiving, prosperity, and family unity begin.

You know that it is coming . . . the part where I insist that you get out your pen and start working on your own thoughts for full moon rituals or celebrations. Full moon rituals do not have to be complicated. No elaborate details, no memorizing lengthy speeches. This is a time for simple celebration and blessings! Be spontaneous. Light a candle or two for the old ones, gather your natural supplies, and speak from your heart.

Now, as promised, here is a fast and easy recipe for esbat (full moon) cookies. This has no eggs in it and the ingredients are usually to be found in the pantry (I don't know about you, but I always seem to be out of eggs whenever I try to bake). This recipe requires no refrigeration time for the dough. If you prefer, substitute all vanilla extract instead of half almond and half vanilla, that works just as well. These make great cookies for any and all occasions. Just mix them up and roll 'em out!

Easy Esbat Mooncakes

¼ cup shortening

¼ cup butter or margarine, at room temperature

¾ cup granulated sugar

¼ cup milk (may need to add a bit more)

½ teaspoon almond extract

½ teaspoon vanilla extract

2 cups flour

1½ teaspoons baking powder

Cream first three ingredients. Add remaining ingredients and mix with spoon. Add more milk if necessary. Roll dough out to ⅛–¼ of an inch thickness on a floured surface and cut into shapes. (Use moon- or star-shaped cookie cutters, or a glass for round shapes.) Bake at 350 degrees for 8–9 minutes on an ungreased cookie sheet (baking times may vary; bake until golden brown on bottom and edges are set). Remove from sheet and carefully transfer to racks or paper towels to cool.

I am the daughter of earth and water,
And the nursling of the sky;
I pass through the pores of the ocean and shores;
I change, but cannot die.

PERCY BYSSHE SHELLEY

Moon Goddesses and Gardening

It is a Wiccan principal that the phases of the moon correspond with the three faces of the Goddess. The Triple Moon Goddess is a foundation of the Wiccan belief system. Moon gardening can be enhanced by aligning yourself with the Moon Goddess in all her aspects.

Each moon phase has its own magickal correlation. You will need to learn for yourself how you, your magick, and your garden react to all three phases.

Work in the increasing moon to pull positive things toward you, such as new projects and health, love, and prosperity. It is a favorable time for blessings and new beginnings, such as a baby, starting a job, or a new house.

The full moon is the time of celebration and attuning with the Goddess. This seven-day phase covers the three days before the full moon, the day of the full moon, and three days following. It is a time of great power that covers all magickal endeavors.

The decreasing moon is to push unwanted things and situations away from you. Removing obstacles are best done in the wane of the moon.

Banishings and bindings should be worked in the dark of the moon. On those three days, the moon is not visible in the sky—the day before, the day of the new moon, and the day afterward.

I have read plenty of magickal books that warn you from working magick in those days of the dark moon. Dangerous, some would say. I disagree. If you work the appropriate magicks during those three days wisely and responsibly, you'll be amazed at the results you achieve.

The pre-Hellenic goddess trinity of Artemis, Selene, and Hecate is a classic pantheon for your moon gardening. Most witches and natural magicians are familiar with these ladies, but don't think about calling on them for gardening. Try working with all three of them. These Greek goddesses were the first I ever worked with as a teen. I discovered them while studying mythology, and was fascinated by their tales. As a trinity of goddesses they are an unbeatable combination. Here are their magickal correspondences, candle colors, and sacred plants.

Artemis, the Maiden

Goddess of the hunt; the guardian of wild places and animals; protector of children and women in childbirth. Artemis despises violence against all women and is the one to call on if you are being hassled or abused by men. After you've removed yourself from the situation, then call on Artemis to help you start a safer, happier, and healthier life.

If you are male, you may want to be cautious and very respectful while working with Artemis. She tended to get a little nasty if she felt she wasn't getting the respect she deserved. There is the story of one poor fellow who accidentally stumbled across Artemis and her companions while they were bathing. Artemis didn't take this very well; she had her dogs and bears tear the man to pieces.

Artemis' candle colors are white and silver. Her plants are the daisy, the herb mugwort (botanical name *Artemesia*), the willow, and the cypress tree. Her influence in the garden will be mostly felt in the early spring and through the month of May. Artemis is often represented as an athletic young woman in a tunic, hunting with a bow. Her crescent moon is to be seen right after sunset in the western sky.

Selene, the Mother

Bride and lover, Selene is the goddess of the full moon. She is the sister of the Sun God Helios. Her sacred day is February 7. Selene's candle colors are white, silver, and gold. Selene specializes in magick . . . all magick. Her trademark talent lies in helping you to find simple solutions to your problems. She will help your garden to grow, your flowers to be prolific, and their blooms to be more sumptuous. Spells for love and romance will also gain special attention from Selene.

Her sacred plants include bluebells, white roses, and moonflowers. Any white- or nighttime blooming flower would fall under Selene's influence as well. Her presence in the garden will be felt on every full moon, and in the growing season of mid-May through September.

Placing a silver gazing globe in the garden would be a great way to acknowledge Selene's presence in your life. Both the silver color and round moon shape would be the perfect accessory. Selene is pictured as a winged, beautiful, gold-crowned woman within the face of the full moon.

Hecate, the Crone

In mythology she is the only Titan who retained her powers after Zeus took over. When other goddess worship declined, the worship of Hecate continued. Also known as Hecate Trevia, Great Goddess of Nature, Queen of the Crossroads, and the Queen of the Witches, she has no comparison in the art of sorcery. An extremely protective goddess, Hecate is mighty and imposing. She watches out for her own.

Festival days include the Festival of Flowers on March 4, which she shares with the goddess Flora. Another is the Night of Hecate on November 16. Hecate's influence is felt in the days of the waning moon, and in the garden season of October through late November.

The garden is gearing down at this time. The crops should all be in. The mums are still blooming, but the roses are fading. Plants start to go dormant and die back as the garden prepares for winter. We are thankful for another good growing season and look forward to our time of rest from the physical side of gardening.

Hecate's candle colors are black and silver. Her sacred plants include mint, the blooming cyclamen, the willow tree (the tree of death), and many poisonous plants. Often pictured as a three-faced goddess bearing a torch or as the quintessential crone in the black cape, her symbols include keys, cauldrons, black dogs, and three-way crossroads.

Interested in more moon goddess information? Do your own research. Go to the library and look through older books on mythology and ancient cultures. Read. Study and learn. You'll be a better witch or natural magician for it.

Magickal Days of the Week and Their Planetary Correspondences

As long as you are studying and learning, the one set of correspondences that I feel *every* witch or magick user should memorize is the daily planetary associations, the coordinating colors assigned to each planet and their magickal uses.

No whining. If I can memorize the basics, I know you can. Committing these planetary correspondences to memory is a promotional step that helps to move you up in the rankings from a newbie witch to an intermediate or advanced practitioner.

Memorize these correspondences:

SUNDAY: Sun, yellow and gold = Success, strength, protection, power

MONDAY: Moon, white and silver = Peace, fertility, love, healing, psychic endeavors

TUESDAY: Mars, red = Passion, sex, power, courage, protection, overthrowing enemies

WEDNESDAY: Mercury, orange = Communication, study, business, wisdom

THURSDAY: Jupiter, purple and blue = Prosperity, money, health, good luck

FRIDAY: Venus, green and pink = Love, romance, beauty, happiness, friendship

SATURDAY: Saturn, black = Banishing, bindings

On to our list of common magickal plants. Remember we are going for the theme of "backyard magick" here, with plants that are both easy to attain and cultivate in your own yards. Match up the planetary correspondences with your magickal intent. Try to memorize as many of the easy plant/planet correspondences as possible, like sunflowers and marigolds for the sun, moonflowers and nicotiana for the moon. Without further ado, here you go. You shouldn't have any problems locating these common plants and flowers. Have fun!

> *People from a planet without flowers would*
> *think we must be mad with joy the whole time*
> *to have such things about us.*
>
> IRIS MURDOCH

Planetary Correspondences for Backyard Magick

SUN: Chamomile, sunflower, marigold, rosemary, daylily, peony, heliotrope, St. John's wort, mums, carnations, rowan tree

MOON: Gardenia, jasmine, mallow, poppy, wintergreen, moonflower, nicotiana, pumpkin, turnip, potato, cabbage, grape, willow tree

MERCURY: Marjoram, parsley, fennel, fern, clover, bergamot, bittersweet, lavender, lily of the valley, dill, aspen tree

MARS: Basil, tarragon, coriander, cilantro, nettle, gentian, snapdragons, radish, holly, hawthorn tree, pine

JUPITER: Hens and chicks, dandelion, meadowsweet, sage, cinquefoil, hyssop, honeysuckle, maple, oak

VENUS: Morning glory, primrose, violet, rose, geranium, tulip, hyacinth, daffodil, daisy, feverfew, foxglove, tansy, strawberry, raspberry, lilac shrubs, birch tree

SATURN: Mullein, ivy, lobelia, morning glory, pansy, Solomon's seal, cypress, elm, mimosa, pine, yew

The idea behind listing all of these correspondences is to help you fine-tune your garden witchery. Let's say that you really needed help in the financial department. Money is tight, some unexpected bill hits, and suddenly you find yourself five days away from payday with twenty dollars in your checking account. (I hate weeks like that.) If you wanted to work for prosperity, your most opportune time would be on a Thursday (that's a Jupiter day) in a waxing moon phase to increase your cash flow or help you stretch things until payday.

Then you would take a peek at the backyard magickal plant list and find those plants that are under Jupiter's influence. Okay, so now you've identified the herbal ingredients that you can easily get your hands on, and you then gather and assemble the components for your spell. Get it?

Now let's talk realistically for a moment. The moon is not always in the phase that we need her to be in for our spells. Sometimes in a pinch you can't sit around and wait for a Jupiter day or a Venus day or even for a whole week for the correct phase of the moon. Sometimes you've gotta go with what you've got.

Back to our prosperity spell, to take another look at how we can work this out. Let's imagine that the moon is on the wane, and it's a Tuesday. Being the clever garden witch that you are, you will check to see how many other elements you could find in sympathy with what you are casting toward.

The moon is waning, so you could banish poverty and your anxiety over the money situation. It's Tuesday, and that's a Mars day. Mars has the attributes of power and courage (we could use some of that). Now you're going to burn a green votive candle for prosperity and a red candle because it's a Mars day. You want those qualities of power and courage for this situation. Assemble as many Jupiter plants together as possible, and go ahead and work the spell anyway. Keep your notes and see how things develop.

I would plan to follow up this prosperity spell with a backup spell on the day and moon phase that would be your most opportune for success. It certainly doesn't hurt to have a backup plan. However, in magick, intent is everything. If you really need to work your magick right away, go for it! Use your brains. Adapt, improvise, and overcome! Take a look at what you have handy at home. There is always a way to magickally work things out.

Garden and Moon Lore

In closing this chapter on all things astrological and lunar, I want to share with you some of my favorite moon and garden lore. Add these to your notebook or Book of Shadows and enjoy!

- A ring around the moon is a warning.

- If a star is caught in soft clouds around the moon, rain will appear and bless the earth.

- When the moon wears a crimson cap, there will be rain, clouds, and unpredictable weather.

- Transplant in the full moon and your flowers are believed to double their usual bloom amounts.

- The full moon in May is a sacred time for gardens and magickal gardening.

- Plant in the first day of the sun sign Virgo, August 22. This is said to have the strongest influence on your plants for bountiful growth.

- The gemstone moonstone is a beneficial one to wear while gardening.

- The gemstone green tourmaline is another stone in harmony with gardening.

- A garden full of lightning bugs is said to be a sign of being blessed by the faeries.

- Ladybugs, a beneficial insect, are sacred to the Fae. A ladybug with seven spots on it is supposed to be a faery pet.

- Leave a few tumbling stones, such as amethyst, tourmaline, quartz crystal, and moonstone, in the garden as a gift to the earth elementals, specifically the gnomes, brownies, and flower faeries. This will ensure a healthy, happy garden.

7

And on the tawny sands and shelves,
Trip the pert fairies and the dapper elves.
JOHN MILTON

Faery Magick

I have met many witches, frustrated with a lack of advanced or intermediate techniques and materials, who turn to faery magick out of the desire to learn something, anything new. There is a certain sense of historical romance about it. Faeries were thought to have whispered herbal remedies to the wisewomen of old.

Nevertheless, faery magick is not to be taken lightly. The realm of the Tuatha de Dannan, the Sidhe, and the Fae is to be approached with respect, courtesy, and caution. It's time for you to do a little research and be specific before you go banging at the doorway to the Faery realm.

Why? Because you are dealing with a whole different realm. Faeries are considered by some to be from the kingdom of the elementals. Others consider them a separate race, known as the Tuatha de Dannan. There are tales that faeries are actually angels who refused to choose sides when Lucifer was rebelling, and so in punishment they were sent forever to the Earth. You will have to decide for yourself who and what you believe them to be.

If you are interested in working with these energies, your best bet would be the garden-friendly gnomes, brownies, and sylphs. Gnomes and brownies are earth elementals. Gnomes are the guardians of the treasures of the earth. They help create plant colors and facilitate the growth of flowers and trees. Gnomes are often perceived to be gnarled, diminutive old men.

Brownies are household fairies. They are said to appear as small, brown, and furry little men. They protect the home, guard your property, and look out for your children and animals. Brownies will also help keep your house clean . . . if you show them kindness.

The sylphs, air elementals, have their own energies and powers. They represent the creative force of the air element: inspiration, intuition, and knowledge. Sylphs appear to us as a classic storybook-type of faery or angel. There are some gentle sylphs and even plant spirits that could pass as a Tinkerbell type of faery—you know, the ones that you've pictured as little air sprites, fluttering about with gossamer wings. Those are the safe sort you'd like to have working with you in the garden. I like to think of them as flower faeries.

Rarely physically seen, these flower faeries make their presence known by walking through your hair or making the leaves on the plants bounce and the petals on the flowers quiver for no apparent reason. They help care for the garden and also enjoy families, pets, and children.

But we must remember that Nature is an entity unto herself. She has many faces, some gentle and others not. The spring breeze that refreshes you can turn into damaging winds during severe thunderstorms. The same creek that babbles by your backyard may do monstrous damage in a flash flood situation. Nature is a paradox. So, too, is the faery realm.

The Good, the Bad, and the Ugly

The Tuatha de Dannan once were treated as gods in pagan Ireland. For instance, these old gods of the earth were at one time so feared it was forbidden to say the word "faery." They were referred to instead as the Gentry or the Good People. The Irish faery beliefs are the most detailed and generally held, and include many types and varieties of faeries. Some are grotesque and almost all are formidable, but what strikes me most of all are the tales of the great beauty of most of the faeries. Over and over we hear legends about their love of music and poetry, faery feasts and rides (or raids), and the beauty of faery women and the faery horses. The Welsh tale of Rhiannon would be a prime example.

Rhiannon's story goes like this. A prince named Pwyll decided to challenge himself by sitting on a hill (faery mound) and tempting fate. Legend stated that any man who sat upon this hill would either receive a "great blow" or see something amazing.

What Pwyll saw was Rhiannon: a beautiful woman in gold, slowly trotting around the hill on a white horse. Captivated, the prince called for his fastest rider to go and fetch the fair maiden, but no matter how fast he went, she was always just ahead and out of reach. Pwyll tried it himself, wearing himself and his horse almost to the point of exhaustion. Still Rhiannon's pace never changed and she remained just ahead of the prince.

Finally, in frustration, the prince called out to Rhiannon and asked the lady to please stop. She did so immediately, and turned to look at Pwyll with amusement. She then told the prince that it would have been better for the horse if he would have but asked her earlier.

For Pwyll it was love at first sight, and he asked Rhiannon to marry him. Rhiannon accepted.

There is thought to be a connection between the realm of the Faery and the dead, but the grandeur of faeries seems to derive from their godlike qualities. In Ireland, more than anywhere else, the faeries are often thought to be shadows of the old gods of the country. In other magickal places, such as Scotland, beliefs are different.

Here the emphasis is placed on the good and the bad among the faeries. Sometimes you will see this referred to as the Seelie and Unseelie courts. I suggest caution. There are many monsters in Scottish faery legend, the kind that come slithering or crawling out of the mist—not to mention the Cailleach Bheur. An aspect of the Crone goddess, the Cailleach is the personification of the typical hunchbacked old crone stirring the smoking cauldron. What does she look like? The Halloween-type, hook-nosed old witch—wise, all-seeing, and a little frightening . . . be careful, my little pretty, or she just might get you too! Some modern authors have described her as being blue-faced and sporting fangs. Now that's downright creepy.

The Cailleach is from the Highlands and she is a more elemental and imposing faery character. The key word here is *elemental*. Do I detect a hint of the old earth gods? It is fascinating how the Cailleach ties into the faery mythology. This is a goddess of the land; the Highlands, to be precise. Today, the Cailleach is a powerful representation of the Crone. Sure, she may be a little scary, but if you approach her wisely and cautiously, you just might learn something.

You need to acknowledge and understand just who and what you are dealing with. The faeries are considered to be good-hearted and merry. Conversely, they are fickle, easily offended, obstinate, and quick to anger. The old beliefs about the dangers surrounding the shifting glamour of Faeryland are ones to take into consideration.

Yes, there are many tales of elven heroism and faery beauty. These fantastic beings are often imagined as suitable for a child's bedtime story, with the traditional tales of enchanting music and their love of sports and revelry. There are also just as many dark legends as well. In reality, try thinking of the Faery kingdom as the good, the bad, and the ugly. You better believe they can still make their presence felt and known.

When I first approached writing this chapter I started to include as much information on the Faery realm as I could find . . . started to, anyway. After a few nights of vivid nightmares, I got the message. A friend pointed out to me that he had heard a story about the poet W. B. Yeats and his search for faery knowledge. Yeats was fascinated by the faery realm, but he was warned by an Irish medium to be careful, and not to seek to know *too* much about the Fae. That's good advice.

Some witches make the mistake of working with the faeries without realizing exactly what they are getting into. Be very particular. If you call them, they will come. I know about this from personal experience.

Faery Mischief and Graveyard Dirt

When I was a young witch and my children were small, I invited in the faeries—specifically, the brownies (house spirits)—to guard the house and yard. I thought the children would love it and I was charmed with the idea. At first, we had a few months of harmless, mischievous pranks. Jewelry started to disappear, car keys went missing, you could leave a room only to walk back a moment later and discover everyday things missing or moved around.

One night I was folding laundry in the living room and I stopped to put the kids to bed. It was one of those wild nights only a parent of several small children could appreciate. Children, toys, and clean laundry scattered all over the floor. The kids were trying to "help," which of course only made it twice as much work.

I hustled the kids into bed and with the three of them safely tucked in, and our old orange tabby cat to keep me company, I started to put away the laundry.

As I walked back into the living room, the laundry basket was gone. I turned around to find it on top of the television. I can honestly say that I had never put the basket up there before. It had been on the rug in the middle of the floor. My heart thudded hard in my throat. I looked down at the cat, who looked up at me as if to say, "Don't look at me."

I scooped up the cat, left the basket untouched and backed out of the room. I walked down the hall to find the kids all still in bed. That was weird, it couldn't have been the kids. I would have seen or heard the kids if they had gotten up. They couldn't have reached the top of the TV at that age, let alone put a full basket up there. My husband worked nights so that left him out, and obviously the cat hadn't done it . . .

Why was the basket on top of the TV? When I walked back into the room to double-check, the basket had moved; it was now on the floor, centered in front of the TV.

I caught movement out of the corner of my eye and turned in time to see something brown and small dart across the floor. The cat in my arms tracked the movement and swung her tail lazily around, but showed no signs of distress. I could feel waves of mischief and fun in the living room. And I knew . . . we had brownies.

During this time we were in the process of building a garden on the side of the house and were besieged with bad luck during our project. We hired someone to remove one hundred feet of old driveway and put in a new, smaller one, a new back porch, and a sidewalk. The kids thought it was great and we were excited . . . I guess the brownies were as well.

The first crew we hired crushed our shed in the backyard and then got mad when we asked them to either pay for a replacement or deduct the cost of the shed from our bill. With hurled obscenities, they walked off the job, leaving the concrete half torn out and our yard looking like a war zone, or a miniature of the Grand Canyon.

After reporting them to the Better Business Bureau, I had to go hire a new, reliable contractor. We found one but had to wait three weeks until he was able to work us in. After he arrived and surveyed the site, he told us we would also have to bring in three dump trucks full of soil for the new side yard, an expense we hadn't planned on.

On the first day the new concrete workers arrived to finish the tear out, they pulled up to get started, only to have to stop an hour later as they mysteriously had two flat tires on their equipment truck. Not one flat tire, but two.

They were embarrassed and had to call a special tow truck to haul away their truck. They left with the promise to return the next day as soon as possible. The owner apologized again for the delay, and repeated how he had never in all his years seen anything like it. Was I cursed or something? he asked.

No, I assured him. But I was beginning to get really suspicious of our "guests." Disappointed and frustrated, I herded the kids back into the house. As the kids and I went back inside, I saw the cat fly down the hall in hot pursuit of something. The kids took off happily after the cat. I sat down and cried.

That night after I put the kids to bed, I looked up ways to counteract faery mischief. There was the theory that they were repelled by iron, and that they disliked cats. I dismissed the latter one, as the brownies didn't seem to mind the cat so far . . . in fact, some texts claimed that cats were faery creatures. Faeries and brownies supposedly love kids and action. We had plenty of that.

I read up on banishing unwanted entities, but that seemed like overkill . . . after all, I had invited them in. So I followed my instincts and sat down to have a little heart-to-heart talk with our brownies. I left them some small crystals by the hearth as a thank-you gift for all their hard work in guarding the house and yard. Then I told them all about the great garden I was planning for them. (Should have done that in the first place.)

I believe that they were only trying to do what I had asked them to do: protect the house and yard. Even though we were in the middle of a landscaping job, the early stages involved a lot of tear-out work. I'm sure to the brownies it seemed like the destruction of our and their home. They probably weren't too thrilled with all that noise and equipment on their turf.

I also did a spell to counteract any bad luck, and then went outside and blessed the yard. To avoid any more equipment problems, I doused any equipment the concrete crew had left behind with sea salt. It worked. The concrete guys finished their work without incident, except they kept accusing each other of eating crackers or pretzels on the truck. The only problem left was to find the dirt for the yard.

When I had given up on finding any affordable topsoil, a neighbor suggested a friend who owned a backhoe. I called him and he quoted me a price that was very inexpensive. The three tons of topsoil was scheduled to arrive the next day, so the concrete workers could move some of it for us with a Bobcat.

Right on time, Mr. Phillips dropped off the first and second dump truck loads. Then he climbed out of the cab, resplendent in his overalls and with a toothpick clenched in his teeth, to inform me that he would be back with the final load later in the afternoon. Before he could return, he had to go to the dentist and then go dig three graves.

The concrete guys stopped working and did a double take; all my neighbors, who had been watching, fell silent; and I just stood there trying not to grin. Mr. Phillips looked uncomfortable and started for the dump truck.

"Hey, Mr. Phillips!" I called after him before he could drive away.

"Yes?" He turned to look at me as I climbed up on the side of the truck so I could see him better.

"By any chance, this dirt wouldn't be graveyard dirt . . . would it?" I asked him.

He turned off the radio and adjusted his cap. He took a deep breath before answering. "Would it bother you if it was?"

"Are you kidding?" I laughed. "As long as there are no body parts in it, bring it on in!" He smiled, relieved, and I climbed down from the truck and waved as he drove away.

My neighbors thought I was taking it awfully well. I thought it was hysterically funny. The concrete guys thought it was great quality dirt at an affordable price, and wanted his name for other jobs. I was happy to pass it along.

My husband said to me when he came home that day, "Well, honey, that kind of goes with the theme, doesn't it?" In a way, I guess it did. I planted the beginnings of my gardens about a week later.

I bet you're wondering if anyone else ever saw the brownies? Actually, yes. Close friends of ours came over to visit and I was telling them about the flat tire incident. As we were sitting around the table visiting, Skippy, our cat, decided to grace us with her presence by jumping on the middle of the kitchen table. She knew she wasn't allowed to do this but, like most cats, she really didn't care about house rules.

I saw movement out of the corner of my eye and, as my husband turned his head to look, our guests both yanked their feet up off the floor in alarm. My friend, Paula, looked at us and said, "Did you guys get another cat?"

"Well, no," I told her. "I think you've just met the brownies."

Her husband, Craig, looked at me and smiled. "You're not talking about the Girl Scouts, are you?"

Faeries in the garden are a wonderful thing. They help care for your plants and protect the garden. If you had invited them into the house and want them to go into the garden instead, they will be more than happy to go. Just politely invite them to move to the garden. Make it a special place for them. Leave gifts, such as crystals, in the garden. Or leave a circle of bread or cookie crumbs under a full moon in thanks for their assistance in the yard.

How will you know if the faeries have moved in the garden? The plants will start to grow more luxuriantly and you will probably find a faery ring in your yard. The circle of mushrooms can be anywhere from three feet wide to much bigger. We had one once that was twenty feet across.

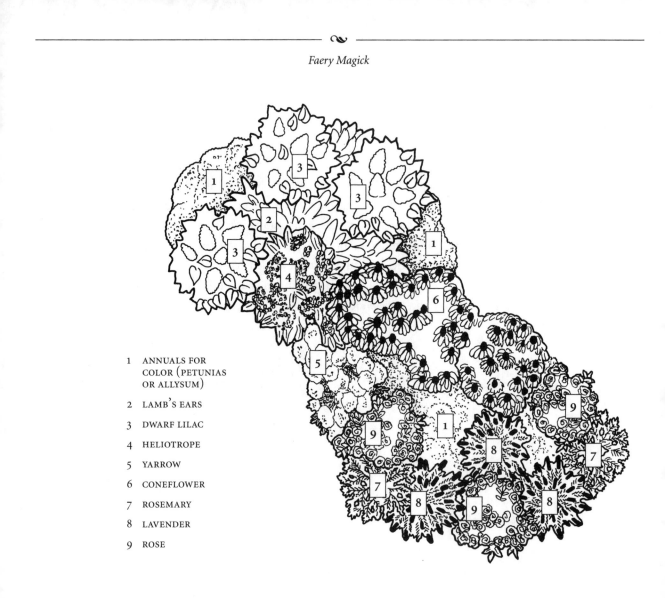

1 ANNUALS FOR
   COLOR (PETUNIAS
   OR ALLYSUM)

2 LAMB'S EARS

3 DWARF LILAC

4 HELIOTROPE

5 YARROW

6 CONEFLOWER

7 ROSEMARY

8 LAVENDER

9 ROSE

A FULL SUN OR FAERY GARDEN LAYOUT

Faery folks are in old oaks.
OLD RHYME

Faery Plants and Garden Plans for Sun and Shade

To attract the flower faeries, try adding these plants to your garden. For the shady garden try ferns, columbine, foxglove, meadowsweet with its wonderful vanilla scent, and lily of the valley. As mentioned before, foxglove and lily of the valley are poisonous plants. You may want to wait until your kids are older before planting these. That's what I did. Forget-me-nots are a faery plant that are rumored to help you in your search for hidden treasures. Violets and lady's mantle are also great shade perennials for a faery garden. Violets are a main faery flower. A chaplet of violets are a charm for love and a shelter from treachery.

For your sunny faery gardens, plant these: lavender, betony (that's lambs ears), yarrow, and rosemary. Train an annual morning glory vine up a trellis and stand back. They grow up to fifteen feet tall in one season. Morning glories are used for all kinds of garden witch spells. Remember, this is another plant you want to make sure your kids don't eat. All parts of the vine, blooms, and the seeds are mildly toxic. You can always try a honeysuckle if you prefer; it's equally favored by the faeries. The lilac shrub is another popular flower with the Fae. There is nothing like the scent of lilacs in the garden.

Add roses in all varieties and colors, the more heavily scented the better. For your children, try growing the miniature variety of roses, sometimes called "fairy roses." They come in all different colors, even green! Add some cherry-scented heliotrope, daisies, and allysum, and what a lovely faery flower garden you'll have!

Enter those enchanted woods,
You who dare.

GEORGE MEREDITH

∾

Faery Times and Places

A charm to call the flower faeries into your garden should be worked on a full moon. The full moon in May is traditionally a opportune time to introduce yourself to the faeries. Other favorable faery days include all the sabbats, with your best times being Ostara, Beltane, and Midsummer.

There is a tradition of working in the between times and places. For example, the beach is neither the ocean nor the land. Likewise a riverbank, or at a crossroads, where two rivers meet . . . are you following me here? We should also mention that places such as natural springs, waterfalls, meadows of wildflowers, pristine woods and wildernesses are the most likely to have faery activity. Faery times of day are just before sunrise, noon, twilight, and midnight.

Suitable oils to be employed in faery spells are lilac and violet. However, the scent of violets makes some people a little queasy. Use it sparingly until you find out how you handle the scent.

There are many deities associated with both the garden and the faeries. You could call on Flora, Roman goddess of flowers; Demeter, the goddess of the harvest; or the trinity of moon goddesses, Artemis, Selene, and Hecate. Feeling romantic? Try the faery queen Titania, or the God in his aspect as the Green Man, or Pan. Behave yourself, now, if you invoke Pan. This lusty god is associated with the nymphs and the satyrs, after all. If you're not comfortable with any of those suggestions, then call on the Great Mother or the Earth Angel to assist you.

I imagine that someone is probably grumbling about my not having included the Goddess Rhiannon or Morgan le Fay. Rhiannon, a faery bride, endured years of torment and hard labor from her own husband and his court from being falsely accused of the murder of their infant son. Eventually Rhiannon was exonerated and restored to her rightful place when the boy was discovered alive and well.

Morgan le Fay was the older sister of King Arthur and the mother of Arthur's only son, the ambitious Mordred. Morgan or Morgaine was either hailed as a priestess and a tragic hero of Avalon, or as an evil temptress with designs for the throne, depending on whose version of the story you believe. So you may want to think carefully about it before you work with these goddesses, as neither of these archetypes led carefree, happy lives.

If you choose to try faery magick, you could build a small altar in the garden. A faery statue nestled into your flowers with a large flat stone in a garden clearing or a small bench is ideal for such a purpose. Make absolutely sure it is a safe place for an open flame. For outside rituals, I like to use tealights with a drop of essential oil on them. I arrange these on a plate when I'm working outside. The flames are small, the candles don't attract unwanted attention from neighbors, and they are portable (I bring the plate inside when I am finished). Never leave a burning candle unattended, especially outdoors.

To begin your get-acquainted ritual, invoke your chosen deity. Leave an offering to the flower faeries, such as a garland of violets, a rose, or small cakes, on your garden altar. Light your candles and speak the following:

> *Gentle flower faeries from near and far, come watch over my backyard.*
>
> *Bless these herbs and fragrant flowers, fill them with your loving power.*
>
> *Late at night when fireflies glow, use your magick to make them grow.*
>
> *By the power of the stars, moon, and sun, do as I will and it harm none.*

When finished, you may choose to meditate for a while or just lie back, sip some wine, and observe the moon and the night sky. Don't forget to bring your candles in when you are finished. Let nature claim the flowers or the food that you left on your altar as an offering.

When the first baby laughed for the first time,
the laugh broke into thousand pieces and they
all went skipping about, and that was the
beginning of fairies.

SIR JAMES BARRIE, *PETER PAN*

Faery Magick and Kids

When you work with the faeries for any length of time, you may start to notice a certain amount of faery mischief in your home. This can be benign or troublesome, depending on the level of faery interest you are receiving. Bottom line, if you practice magick and you have kids, you are going to attract the attention of the faeries. If you have children who have a natural flair for magick, you're in for even more interesting times.

When our old orange tabby cat died a few years ago, the whole family was heartbroken, my daughter especially, as Skippy had been "her cat." Our other cat, a young gray and black tabby, was lonely without Skippy, but we all decided to wait a while before adopting another animal into the family.

My daughter, Kat, was not so patient. After a few weeks it seemed like every time I opened the door, a different friendly stray cat would be sitting on my front porch—harmless, cute, curious, and wanting a good scratch. My daughter was only too happy to oblige. I warned the kids to be careful and not to feed any strays, and assumed that would be the end of it. A few days later I arrived home from work to find my daughter sitting in the back yard with a big fluffy orange cat on her lap. After the initial double-take, when I assured myself that it was not our Skippy, I went outside to ask her about her new friend.

The cat had a collar and actually belonged to a family down the street. No, we could not keep him, I told her. However now that he had found a soft touch, that fluffy cat was back every day. For a month this neighbor would sit outside under the kitchen window and meow loudly until Kat came outside to hold him and play with him. This continued all summer until the family that he belonged to moved away. When the parade of strays suddenly resumed once again, I took my daughter aside and reminded her that it was okay to miss her pet. I then gently asked her if she had been working any magick.

Her face turned red, and she started to laugh nervously at her spell's success. Kat admitted that she had asked the faeries to send us another cat. And they certainly had, every stray in the neighborhood. "What do we do now?" she asked me.

That evening, the two of us performed a small ritual to thank the faeries for helping, but to please stop sending any more cats to us for now. The parade of strays stopped immediately.

I bet you're wondering if my daughter ever managed to get another pet? Yes, she did. About a year later, my family adopted a stray kitten from the animal shelter in our neighborhood. We ended up with a sleek, solid black feline with bright yellow eyes. She adores my daughter and follows Kat everywhere.

Sometimes faery mischief gets a little out of hand. Signs to look for are a suspicious string of small annoyances or bad luck—missing jewelry that will then turn up in odd places, skittish household pets, and a house that never seems at rest or calm, even after the kids go to sleep.

A witch that I know, Crystal, has a young daughter who possesses a real knack for calling in the faeries. Missy is a natural. At the tender age of eleven, this young girl possesses as much information and experience of working with faery energy as most adult practitioners that I know.

Unfortunately, it tended to create havoc with any and all spells that her mother performed. The entire house and yard was a hotbed of mischievous faery activity. Guest's car keys would disappear, and the house had an unsettled, jumpy feeling, way beyond what you would expect in a house full of small children. When our group put their heads together, we came up with a way to minimize the trouble her daughter was causing, albeit unknowingly.

The first thing we did was to have Crystal cleanse the house and perform a banishing. As a single mom she was the head of the house, and if anyone could do a little faery busting, it should be her. I had her take some salt and water and asperge the four corners of the house and announce that any unknown spell or purpose not in alignment with herself should depart.

Why? Because by announcing that any magick other than her own had to go, she cleaned up any extra bits of magickal energy that might have been floating around, causing chaos. I encouraged her to remind her daughter to take down any circles that she was casting—no sense in having a bunch of trapped, pissed-off elementals hanging around the house. They had enough nature spirit activity in there already.

As a group, we all tried to teach Missy some faery etiquette. Nicole (another adult member of the group, who is herself very talented with nature spirits) gently reminded Missy to be very careful with the faeries. Nicole and I both warned Missy that the Fae are infamous for stirring up trouble and causing mischief, just for the sheer joy of it. It is simply their way. Nicole had a personal stake in this, as it was always her keys that would disappear! They turned up in the weirdest places on circle night. I would watch her put her keys in her purse and then later, when it was time to go home, they were usually gone.

Crystal performed her cleansing and it worked out very well. The animals are calmer and friendlier, and her house is a much more relaxing place to be. It now has a welcoming, I'm-so-glad-you're-here feeling. So the moral of these stories are (and all good faery tales have a moral): Don't allow your children free rein with faery magick. Supervise them if possible, or you may find yourself in some faery-mayhem situations. Remember to teach your children that if they work with faeries to always make sure they work inside of a cast circle. More importantly, remind them to take down their circles when they are finished. Encourage the fairies to live outside in the garden and everyone will be happier.

My teenage daughter Kat helped me to write these next faery spells. She went over this entire chapter's spells and charms with all of the relentless enthusiasm of a drill sergeant. I dedicate this chapter to her because she always insisted, rather loudly, that I should tell our faery stories.

Do you seek the road to fairyland? I'll tell; it's easy, quite.
Wait till a yellow moon gets up o'er purple seas by night
And gilds a shining pathway that is sparkling diamond bright
Then, if no evil power be nigh to thwart you out of spite,
And if you know the very words to cast a spell of might,
You get upon a thistledown and, if the breeze is right,
You sail away to Fairyland along this track of light.

ERNEST THOMPSON SETON

❧

Faery Spells

Spell for Faery Protection of Your Property

For this spell, you will need:

- A small, attractive faery or gnome statue to place in your garden, to represent their benevolent presence on the property

- A few tealights

- Violet or lilac oil (just a drop or two)

- A posy, or small bouquet of flowers that are sacred to the faeries

- Timing: In a waxing or full moon. Work on a Monday for the moon's psychic influence. Chant the following spell three times:

Small garden faeries, brownies, and gnomes,

Come circle 'round and protect my home.

A token of friendship I now leave in this place

May you always guard and defend this sacred space.

Stopping Faery Mischief in the Home

To work this spell, you will need:

- A tealight

- Patchouli oil (a drop or two on the candle)

- A half cup of graveyard dirt—if you can't discreetly get your hands on some, you may substitute dried, crushed mullein leaves

- Iron cauldron, any size. Put the graveyard dirt in the cauldron. Place a tealight inside of the cauldron, on top of the dirt. If you use dried mullein leaves, sprinkle them in a circle going in a widdershins direction around the *outside* of the cauldron. (For safety, do not have dry ingredients near an open flame.)

- Timing: On a full moon for power; during the waning moon for a banishing; and in the dark of the moon if you are in *way* over your head. Work on a Friday (Venus' day) if you are asking them to leave nicely. Choose a Saturday, Saturn's day, for a full-blown banishing, should the situation be intense. Repeat this spell three times.

That's quite enough trouble, it's time now to cease,

Halt your Fae mischief, cause no more faery grief.

With love I release you, go safely on your way,

Return to the garden to sing, dance, and play.

Take out your garden witchery notebook or use this book's journal and jot down your ideas for a faery garden, and note any faery plants that may already be growing in your yard.

(Don't overlook those violets!) Make a wish list for some new enchanting plants and add them into your garden as soon as you are able.

Nature spirits are shy and may take some time before they will make their presence known to you. Be patient. You will probably sense them long before you ever catch a glimpse of them. Pay attention as you work in your garden. I have watched with held breath as the flowers quivered or a tree limb bounced, for no other obvious reason, as I spoke to a plant or tree. The faeries may make their presence known in a variety of ways.

Even I, who have worked with the garden faeries for many years, was surprised to have been awoken late one Beltane night to the sound of what could only be described as faery music. Drifting through the window, first loud and then soft, came the unbelievable combination of whispers, flutes, and bells. Coming fully awake, I raced to the bedroom window to try and pinpoint the source of that sound. As I stood there, I began to realize the sound was definitely coming from somewhere out in the garden. Did I rush outside to investigate? No, I accepted it as the extraordinary gift that it was, for I knew that to intrude would be disrespectful. I climbed back into bed and happily burrowed under the covers just to listen, leaving the faeries to their own revelry.

8

*I have never had so many good ideas, day after
day, as when I worked in the garden.*

JOHN ERSKINE

ᘒ

GARDEN WITCH CRAFTS

This chapter puts the "craft" back into your witchcraft. Are you ready to put a whole new spin on the arts and crafts store? I'll warn you now, you'll never look at a craft store the same way again after I get through with you.

We are going to explore making magickal accessories. You'll find directions on how to sew some drawstring-style charm bags and magickal herbal-scented dream pillows, as well as recipes for magickal sachets to fill those charm bags and pillows. There are instructions for fashioning dried tussie-mussie bouquets. We'll look at formulas for bath salts, suggestions for herbal wreaths, and thoughts on creating your own garden witch's Book of Shadows. This chapter will finish with a small correspondence chart of backyard flowers and plants, including everyday herbs that you probably have in your cupboards and their magickal uses, as well as crystal and color correspondence tables.

Magickal accessories such as pillows are an easy, inexpensive project to start out with, even for those of us who shudder at the sight of a sewing machine. My sewing skills are basic at best, limited to pillows, craft projects, hemming the occasional pair of shorts, and, of course, the yearly Halloween costumes.

Botanical, celestial, and Halloween fabrics are fun to work with for your projects. Sometimes the celestial or astrological prints may be found in the juvenile section. In the fall, when they put out the winter holiday fabrics, you can usually find prints in deep purple and blue with metallic stars and such. Watch for sales or check the bargain tables.

I will confess that I am always on the lookout for Halloween fabric. I've made vests, table cloths, throw pillows, and, of course, many charm bags out of Halloween material. Halloween fabrics featuring adorable folk-art witches, full moons, stars, and cats usually start to show up in stores around July. Some fabric stores will carry it year 'round, but they will have a bigger selection in the late summer months.

I think charm bags that are sewn up from fabric that has witches and other magickal themes on them are fun and clever. They're *charm* bags, after all. For those anal-retentive types who consider Halloween fabrics that sport cute little girl witches with pumpkins and cats beneath them, or harvest-theme material that feature witches on brooms and stirring cauldrons in bad taste . . . I say, oh, loosen up. You are allowed to laugh and enjoy your witch-craft, you know. Tuck that tongue firmly in your cheek and let's have some fun, shall we?

> *What is charm? It is what the violet has*
> *and the camellia has not.*
> FRANCIS MARION CRAWFORD

Charm Bags

Charm bags are a classic example of a garden witch craft. With a few simple ingredients found around the house, some fabric, a bit of ribbon, herbs from the garden, and the secret added power of the garden witch, you have the makings of a potent magickal tool.

Often the simplest and easiest magicks, such as a charm bag filled with magickally charged herbs and stones, will work the best. Small and easily portable, they make wonderful magickal talismans for all kinds of situations: for good luck on job interviews, healing after a surgery, keeping ghosts out of a home, or increasing sales at a business—just about anything you can think of.

A good illustration of the charm bag would be one that I made for a coworker who traveled all the time but was actually afraid to fly. This charm bag included a moonstone for safe travel and some homegrown lavender and a few drops of the essential oil for its calming effects. I tossed in some sea salt to banish negativity and added yarrow for courage. I passed it along with instructions to keep the bag on his person or in his carryon bag. After returning from his trip, it was reported back to me that it was the smoothest flight he had ever taken and that he was even bumped up to first class!

Sewing Directions for Drawstring Charm Bags

1. Cut out two fabric pieces into 4 x 6-inch sections. Press under ¼ inch across the shorter side.

2. To make the drawstring channel, fold over the fabric again ½ inch. Press. Sew right above the folded edge. Make sure you are allowing enough room for a ribbon to pass through. Repeat on the second section of fabric.

3. Turn both pieces so the right sides are facing each other. Pin in place.

4. Sew ⅛-inch seams across the bottom and the sides, stopping just before your seam along the top folded edge. Clip corners. Turn right-side out and press.

5. Cut twelve inches of a coordinating ribbon and pull through the seam allowance, across the top of both sides of the bag, with a safety pin. Cut the ribbons at an angle to help avoid fraying. Pulling on both ribbons will draw the bag tightly closed.

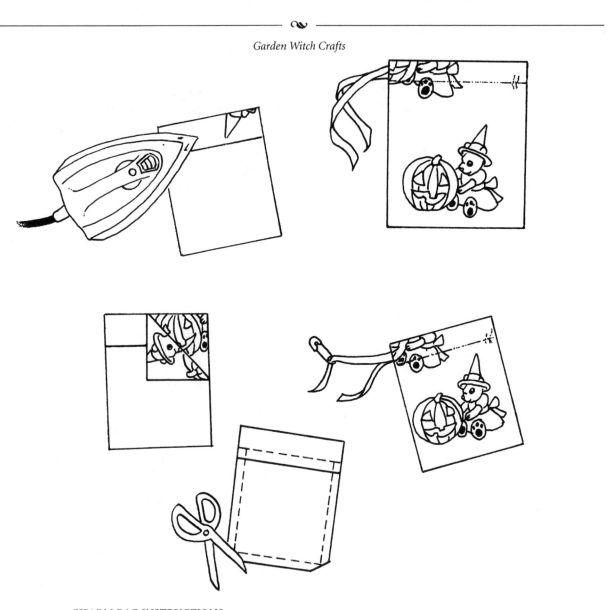

CHARM BAG INSTRUCTIONS

Now, to fill those charm bags using ideas listed under Recipes for Spellbinding Sachets on page 146. The ingredients are given in the following order: charm bag color, suggested herbs, and suggested crystals. In regards to the crystals, use those small, inexpensive tumbling stones that you can pick up at any metaphysical or nature-type store.

Choose your ingredients, and place them into the charm bag. Draw the ribbon up tightly to close the bag. Empower the magickal sachet by holding it in both hands and visualizing what it is that you want it to do. Then, using an old Craft standby, tie the charm bag shut and knot the ribbon three times, saying:

> *By the powers of the moon* (tie the first knot)
>
> *The stars* (tie the second knot)
>
> *And the sun* (tie the third knot)
>
> *Do as I will, an' it harm none.*

Or, if you prefer, you may try this:

> *By the powers of the Maiden* (knot)
>
> *The Mother* (knot)
>
> *And the Crone* (knot)
>
> *Bless this charm bag that I have sewn.*

DREAM PILLOW DIRECTIONS

To sleep: perchance to dream . . .
SHAKESPEARE

Dream Pillows

Dream pillows are small, decorative pillows filled with stuffing and a small amount of dried, fragrant herbs, such as lavender or rose petals, to promote restful sleep or love. These make a fun and easy project for a beginner or for a teen. Celestial fabrics and botanical prints in particular are delightful choices for dream pillows.

1. Cut your dream pillow fabric into 6½-inch squares. Place the right sides of the fabric together.

2. Sew shut three of the sides of the pillow using a ⅛-inch seam allowance. On the final and fourth side, sew the seams in one inch on both sides, leaving the center open to receive stuffing.

3. Turn pillow right-side out, work out the corners to a point, and press.

4. Stuff the pillow with fiberfill and add a few tablespoons of dried herbs.

5. If you care to use an essential oil, use one drop in the center of the stuffing. Don't go overboard on the oils. It will stain the pillow and, if the scent is too strong, it may make the recipient nauseous. A light scent is desirable, nothing more.

6. Sew the pillow shut by hand. Pin the raw edges together, turning them to the inside, and then whipstitch the pillow closed with matching thread.

To enchant your dream pillow, say this verse while you sew the pillow shut:

By the powers of magick and flowers grown,

Bless this dream pillow that I have sewn.

Secure your seam with three knots and snip the thread on the last verse.

Note: Please be careful and do not use any herb or oil that may be toxic, especially if you are giving this pillow to a older child or pregnant woman. If this is a gift for a child, make sure that they are old enough not to eat the contents.

Some safe herbs, fragrant flowers, and spices to use in dream pillows are lavender for peace; rose petals for love and romance; chamomile flowers to soothe and uplift; calendula blooms promote good health; mint leaves encourage prosperity and are refreshing; dried, grated orange rind and lemon rind will perk you up and boost your energy; and rose geranium leaves are for elegance and devotion.

Recipes for Spellbinding Sachets

These sachets may be inserted into either charm bags or dream pillows.

CONCEPTION: Pastel yellow for creativity (tie up the bag with blue and or pink ribbons); yarrow, rosebuds, cyclamen leaf or bloom for fertility; acorns for a boy and cinquefoil for a girl (add both if you aren't particular); rose quartz for love; and a moonstone for the Goddess' assistance.

GOOD LUCK: Green and gold; a four-leaf clover, mint, cinquefoil, basil, and an oak or maple leaf for prosperity and good fortune; aventurine is the gambler's stone.

LOVE: Pink and red; red rose petals, yarrow, and rosemary for love; a maple leaf to sweeten things up; rose quartz for love. Note: Don't target anyone specifically, use this to draw love to you.

PEACE: Blue or light purple; angelica, lavender flowers, and pink rose petals for peace and healing; an amethyst and moonstone for their protective and calming qualities.

PICK-ME-UP: Orange or yellow; bergamot, dried orange, and lemon peel, and mint to refresh you; carnation petals for energy; tiger's-eye and carnelian for passion and courage.

PROSPERITY: Green or gold; cinnamon sticks, cinquefoil, mint, and pine to attract money; aventurine and malachite brings fortune and prosperity.

PROTECTION: Black or purple; periwinkle vine, garlic, morning glory vine, and dill for protection; sea salt to banish bad vibes; a hematite stone for grounding and destressing; an obsidian for protection and courage.

PSYCHIC POWER: Purple or silver; cyclamen, violets, a rowan leaf, and lilac leaf or flower to promote psychic abilities; a black feather for mystery; a quartz crystal for power; and a moonstone to encourage empathy.

SAFE TRAVEL: Blue or white; yarrow for courage; lavender for its calming influences; sea salt to break up negativity; moonstone is a safe travel stone.

STUDY AND KNOWLEDGE: Orange, lily of the valley, lavender, fennel, dill, and sage for wisdom; clematis for mental beauty; carnations for stamina; and quartz crystal for power.

Gently steep our spirits, carrying with them
dreams of flowers.

WILLIAM WORDSWORTH

Yarrow Love Charm

The following is an adaptation of a flower spell from the 1800s. To perform this enchantment you must gather an ounce of yarrow blossoms and sew them into a small flannel bag. I would cut the fabric no larger than a three-by-five-inch piece. Either sew it up on a sewing machine or whipstitch it together by hand. Red or pink would be the fabric color to use for this charm bag and for the ribbons to tie it closed.

The entire spell, the gathering of the herb, and the sewing of the charm bag should be worked on the night of the full moon. After tying up the bag, place it beneath your pillow. Repeat this incantation, while gazing at the full moon, before bedtime.

Thou lovely herb of Venus' tree,

Thy true name is yarrow;

Now who will my true love be?

Pray tell thou me tomorrow.

In olden times this was said to ensure that a maiden would dream of her future husband. A creative, clever witch would take one look at this old charm and then wonder how they could further enhance it. There are all sorts of ways to spice this spell up!

How about burning a spicy-scented pink votive candle dressed with rose oil to ensure a little passion? You may try jasmine or ylang-ylang oil. Add a rose quartz stone to effect love and a carnelian to encourage desire. For information on impending romantic possibilities or even a glimpse of your future spouse, carve a question mark and a heart on the sides of the candle. Sweet dreams!

Tussie-Mussie in a Teacup

Take an old, castoff teacup and some colorful dried flowers, and turn them into an enchanting little gift for a friend or for yourself. In chapter 4 we discussed the tussie-mussie. Now, armed with the knowledge of the language of flowers and using dried flowers, you can turn that inspiration into a fun little magickal project.

Pick out some pretty dried flowers and get started. These bouquets are meant to be diminutive, so you don't have to go crazy and purchase tons of dried flowers. Small amounts will do very nicely. Try using different colored dried roses, fragrant lavender, and hydrangea blooms. Work with golden yarrow, poppy pods, and nigella. Brightly colored cockscomb, purple statice, and tawny-colored wheat stalks will add texture.

Supplies:

Dried flowers of your choosing

Small bag of green sheet moss

An old castoff china teacup

Floral foam cut to fit the teacup

Knife

Floral pins

Scissors

Hot glue gun and glue sticks

1. Cut the foam to fit down snugly into your teacup.

2. Use a thin sheet of the moss to completely cover up the foam. Secure with a floral pin or two. Make tiny clusters of dried blooms and then, using the scissors, trim the stems of dried materials to same length. Insert the stems of the first little bundle into the center of the foam.

3. Working out from the center of the cup, continue adding flowers in clusters, positioning shorter flowers and stems near the edges so that the arrangement rolls over the rim. Some flowers may require a bit of hot glue to help hold them into place. Keep the bunches of flowers close together. You want the flowers in this arrangement to be packed tightly together.

Note: Don't be afraid to use an old teacup or creamer that is less than perfect. If it is chipped or cracked, so much the better. It adds character. Watch flea markets and garage sales for inexpensive old teacups, saucers, and creamers. Dried flowers are to be found at most arts and crafts stores. Try checking with an herb or potpourri shop for more exotic options. If your garden isn't producing anything or you need more supplies, check the arts and crafts store.

*I have had a good many more uplifting
thoughts, creative and expansive visions
while soaking in comfortable baths,
than I ever had in any cathedrals.*

EDMUND WILSON

ꬿ

Bedazzling and Bejeweled Bath Salts

Bath salts are a pleasant project for a beginner. Some sea salt or Epsom salts, a little essential oil, some dried herbs, and violà! Place your salts into some funky glass jars that you can purchase at a home interior store, or sterilize and then use old baby food jars. Add small seashells to the salts or embellish the jars by tucking in a few tumbling stones—be as crafty as you like! A basic recipe for bath salts is as follows:

1 cup sea salt or Epsom salt

Several drops of essential oil (any kind)

A few drops of food coloring

A resealable bag

Put salt, oils, and food coloring in the resealable bag, and press air any out. Seal the bag and massage the contents until they are well blended. Place into airtight, nonporous container and store in a dark, cool place for three days. After the salts have cured, place into a glass jar. Use 2–3 tablespoons per bath. When using food coloring to tint the salts, less is more. You could turn the bathtub or your skin colors if you use too much.

Bath salts will cause your pores to open up and you may perspire. If you use too much salts in the bath, it may make you lightheaded. Be conscientious of skin allergies, and if you are pregnant or nursing you may want to avoid using bath salts altogether. Try sprinkling the water with a small amount of fresh rose petals or lavender buds instead.

SEA SIREN: 5 drops of jasmine oil, 1 tablespoon of powdered kelp (available at health food stores), a few drops of blue food coloring to tint the salts. Add a few tiny seashells to your jar when finished for a charming gift.

GARDEN WITCH: 2 drops of rose oil, 3 drops of lavender oil, and 1 drop of orange oil. Add 3 tablespoons of dried lavender flowers and sprinkle in some dried pink rose petals. This bath salt would be pretty tinted a soft purple or pink.

CLAIRVOYANT CLEANSING: 4 drops of lilac oil and 3 drops of lavender oil. Tuck into the jar a few amethyst tumbling stones or sprigs of dried lavender. Tint a soft purple. Good for a cleansing after a lot of psychic work, or for when you just have had one hell of a day. This will help clear the aura and clean off any negativity that you are still carrying around.

MAGICK MAN (JUST FOR THE GUYS): 4 drops patchouli oil and 3 drops rosemary oil; add a few drops of green food coloring. This has a resinous, pine-forest-type scent.

WIZARD'S BLEND (FOR GUYS AND GALS): 3 drops of orange oil, 2 tablespoons grated, dried orange peel, and a fresh sage leaf, chopped fine. The sage is for wisdom and the orange for purification. Add a quartz crystal for power.

PASSIONATE PRACTITIONER: With this recipe, you should blend or adjust the amounts to your preference. Omit or add more drops of any of these oils to suit: 2 drops rose oil, 1 drop lavender oil, 1 drop ylang-ylang, and 2 drops jasmine oil. A rose quartz crystal or two would be nice. Finally, add red rose petals for romance and tint these salts pink.

RHIANNON'S REFRESHER: 3 drops of orange oil, 3 drops of mint oil, and 1 drop of neroli oil. You may add 1 tablespoon of grated, dried orange peel to this mixture for texture and color. Add a small piece of moonstone or citrine to these salts. You can figure out what color to tint the salts.

> *You can't use up creativity.*
> *The more you use, the more you have.*
> MAYA ANGELOU
> ∽

Magickal Herbal Wreaths

Wreath making is an ancient practice. The ancient Romans used wreaths to celebrate Saturnalia, a winter solstice celebration, and the wreath has been employed since the Middle Ages to celebrate the changing seasons and holidays. Creating an enchanted herbal wreath is an enjoyable process. There are three basic elements to wreath making: the base, the materials used, and the method of attachment. It's not expensive or difficult to do. Many of the necessary items you may either have on hand, could grow yourself, or can be found easily at your local arts and crafts store. Basic supplies you will need include:

A glue gun and glue sticks

Florist wire, 20 gauge

Floral picks

A base wreath (try a grapevine, straw, pine, or a moss wreath)

Dried or fresh flowers, seed pods, nuts, small twigs, and feathers

Ribbons in assorted widths and colors

First, take a walk around the yard and see how you can use the bounty that your garden has to offer. The garden has much to provide: herbs and flowers, changing autumn leaves, acorns, pine cones, twigs, and fallen feathers. Often a lazy hour spent outdoors scavenging yields more organic material than any trip to the store. Please recall those gathering guidelines from chapter 2, and get permission if you are harvesting natural materials on someone else's property. Be a courteous gatherer.

When you begin to assemble the components for your own wreaths, you may want to refer to the correspondence chart listed at the end of the chapter. Don't forget your intuition, though. Let your instincts guide you.

Lay the wreath out first. Take your time and arrange things to your liking. Have fun, relax, and enjoy yourself. Remember that it's much easier to shift pieces around *before* you glue them on than it is to pry them off afterward. If you are incorporating twigs or viny things like bittersweet into the wreath, try to work them into the grapevine for a more natural look.

You may use different colors of ribbon to decorate the wreath or to weave a pentagram inside of the circle. Experiment with coordinating colors for certain needs and to align with the elements.

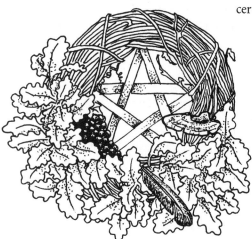

Ready to get started? Before I turn you loose, here are several seasonal projects for you to try and to get the creative juices flowing. These projects are meant to be a starting point for you. Change them around and add to them according to your tastes.

SPRING WREATH: A moss wreath would be an interesting choice for the base, or a grapevine. Add silk lilacs and dried rosebuds. If the wreath is going to be for Ostara, try tulips and daffodils, and use dried baby's breath and yarrow for fillers. Tuck a tiny faery in your wreath so she's peeking out from the flowers. A decorative bluebird with a tiny nest would be very spring oriented. You could add some mini garden tools or tie on a tiny watering can.

LAMMAS WREATH: I like a straw wreath for the base, it seems more summer oriented. Decorate this wreath with sunflowers, either dried or silk. Add stems of wheat, black feathers, or a small decorative silk blackbird. Use dried yellow yarrow from the garden, marigolds, and purple statice, which looks great with these colors as a filler.

HARVEST OR SAMHAIN WREATH: Begin with a large grapevine wreath. Add dried golden yarrow, red cockscomb, and miniature ornamental corn. See if you can work in a few miniature pumpkins or gourds. (Use floral picks for the heavier items and glue them in securely.) Weave in bittersweet or rose hips and dyed oak leaves. Embellish with a few gilded acorns. For Samhain, weave an orange or black pentagram into the center of the wreath.

YULE WREATH: A live or artificial pine wreath as the base is traditional. Pine cones add texture and are easy to find. Add sprigs of holly, dried rose hips, seed pods, nuts, and acorns. Small twigs spray painted white and then sprinkled with iridescent glitter are a sparkling addition. Add a silk red bird (cardinal) to your wreath. How about a partridge and a few small artificial pears? Lastly, tie on some bundles of cinnamon sticks for a prosperous new year.

It doesn't matter whether you grew the herbs and flowers in your own garden and dried them yourself, found them while scavenging, or bought them in the craft store. There are many resources for materials. Searching is half the fun. Enjoy creating your magickal wreaths and keep your eyes open for those little treasures of nature. The Goddess is eternally bountiful. Walk gently, open your heart, and see what you find. Happy wreath making!

A Garden Witch's Book of Shadows

Now that you have all these wonderful creative ideas and spells swirling around in your brain, where are you going to put them? I hope you have been writing your own charms and recipes. I bet you went out and made a faery garden, didn't you? How did it go? Did you notice any changes in the yard? In your magick? Are we keeping track?

Remember that spiral notebook that you started taking your first garden witch notes in? Let's jazz it up a little and make it into a garden witch's Book of Shadows. A Book of Shadows is simply a witch's recipe book—a listing of notes, correspondences, and tried-and-true favorites.

Every BOS is unique, as is each witch or natural magician. The difference here will be that we are going to be adding plant information and our gardening notes. Sounds like another excuse to be magickally creative, doesn't it ?

Either use a binder or locate a blank book or journal. This is your magickal journal, so make it however you want it. Try writing out your spells and recipes with different colored pens and decorating the pages with rubber stamp art. Magickal themes such as faeries, witches, and wizards are classic. Keep your eyes open for Halloween rubber stamps and stickers too.

If you go the three-ring binder route, check out the scrapbook sections at the craft store and look for interesting computer paper to print your spells out on. Take a look at celestial, floral, and garden motif stickers for embellishing the pages.

Add photos from your own gardens, pictures of your spouse, children, or pets, and anything that is special to you. Clip out flower photos, gardening quotes, and magazine articles on gardening and plant folklore that appeal to you and glue them in (I recommend using a glue stick for this).

I don't advise placing dried, pressed flowers in the journal, unless you put clear contact paper over them. I tried to glue dried, pressed pansies in my BOS once. They looked great until I closed the book and the flowers crumbled apart. It made a hell of a mess altogether.

Your garden witch BOS may be used to record gardening trials and triumphs: what plants grew well, which plants sulked, varieties that you'd like to try next year, and so on.

Basically, your garden witch BOS should reflect you. Take your time and build your BOS up slowly over the years. If you want it to be more gothic and witchy, try your hand at calligraphy and go for it! If you enjoy a botanical theme, or happen to have a thing for flower stickers (which I am guilty of), indulge yourself.

All of the projects in this chapter are designed for you to have a little fun experimenting with the crafty side of witchcraft. Go ahead, try your hand at being artistic. No one is going to grade you. Do you think all of my craft projects, magickal or otherwise, turned out splendidly over the years? Wait a minute, I have to glare at my husband for laughing at me.

Anyway, be daring! Live, laugh, and learn. Most of all, just enjoy the creative process!

> *Laugh, and the world laughs with you.*
> *Sing . . . and the hills will answer.*
>
> ELLA WHEELER

At-a-Glance Plant Correspondences

Prosperity
COLOR: Green. ELEMENT: Earth. PLANTS: Acorns, bayberry, bergamot, cinnamon, cinquefoil, heliotrope, honeysuckle, mint, nuts, oak leaves, pine, poppy, tulip, wheat

Love
COLOR: Red. ELEMENT: Fire. PLANTS: Catnip, clove, dill, geranium, lady's mantle, meadowsweet, orange rind, pansy, rosemary, rose, rose hips, tiger lily, violet, yarrow

Healing
COLOR: Blue. ELEMENT: Water. PLANTS: Angelica, bittersweet, carnation, geranium, juniper, lavender, meadowsweet, mullein, oak, rosemary, rue, St. John's wort, tansy, thyme

Creativity
COLOR: Yellow. ELEMENT: Air. PLANTS: Aspen, grapevine, horehound, iris, lavender, lily of the valley, nutmeg, periwinkle, rosemary, rue, sage, spearmint, sunflower, wisteria

Protection
COLOR: Black. ELEMENT: All. PLANTS: Betony, cloves, cypress, dill, foxglove, garlic, hydrangea, rose geranium, rowan twigs, rue, snapdragons, yarrow, sweet woodruff, violet

At-a-Glance List for Crystal and Stone Magick

AMETHYST: Peace and psychic power—a good stone to keep with your Tarot cards

AVENTURINE: The gambler's stone, prosperity, and good luck

BLOODSTONE: Health, good luck, and healing

CARNELIAN: Love, lust, and health

CITRINE: Psychic abilities

HEMATITE: Grounding and healing

LAPIS LAZULI: Healing, love, psychism, bravery; this stone is sacred to the Goddess Isis

LEPIDOLITE: Peace, protection, and brings good luck in new ventures

MOONSTONE: The Goddess, moon magick, safe travel, self-analysis

MALACHITE: Cash, business success, healing, and protection

OBSIDIAN: Grounding, deflects negativity, and protection

QUARTZ CRYSTAL: Power, this will magnify any other crystal or stone added to the charm bag

ROSE QUARTZ: Love, self-confidence, friendships, and warm fuzzies

TIGER'S-EYE: Protection and success

TURQUOISE: Protection and healing, friendship and good luck

Magickal Color List

I thought this index might come in handy for all of your garden witch craft projects. As you choose fabric for your charm bags or decorate your wreaths with assorted colored ribbons, you may care to refer to this magickal color list. Note: This is also a handy reference guide for candle magick.

RED: Passion, love and healing, the element of fire, and the Mother Goddess

ORANGE: Energy, action, communication, and intensity

YELLOW: Creativity, conception, studying, spring, and the element of air

GREEN: Prosperity, healing, gardening, herbalism, faery magick, and the element of earth

BLUE: Peace, hope, healing, and the element of water

PURPLE: Psychic powers, to increase personal power, and magick

BROWN: Grounding, happy homes, pets, and garden magick

BLACK: Breaking hexes, banishing illness or negativity, and the Crone

WHITE: All-purpose, the Maiden Goddess, peace, calm, and hope

GREY: Bindings, banishing, invisibility spells, and glamouries

SILVER: The Goddess, women's mysteries, the moon, and intuition

GOLD: The God, riches, wealth, and fame

PINK: Love, warm fuzzies, friendship, and children

BABY BLUE: Comfort, children, and harmony

LIME GREEN: Warding off jealousy, seed blessing, and springtime magick

LILAC: Clairvoyance, Tarot work, and faery magick

9

My mom's a witch and my uncle
married the Easter bunny . . .

A FAVORITE FAMILY SAYING AT MY HOUSE

∞

Sabbat Celebrations for Families

True statement. Seriously, it is. During an Easter Sunday brunch celebrated at my parent's home several years ago, my mom and dad thought it would be the most wonderful idea to go and visit my brother and his fiancée while they worked at an Easter buffet. My parents wanted the kids to be there specifically because my brother's fiancée, who stands just at five feet tall, was going to be dressed up as the Easter bunny.

My children were less than thrilled. There was that coolness factor to be considered, after all. They were too old to believe in the Easter bunny. My husband and I had to watch them carefully that year, to make sure that they didn't make any comments about how colored eggs and the white rabbit were actually archaic symbols for the Goddess of Spring. Some Pagan kids hit that age and are ready to tell *anybody* who will listen what those Christian holidays are actually based on. (You know, just to prove to others how smart they really are.) Well, at the time, all three of mine were going through that phase.

So we loaded up the troops and off we went to the hotel where my brother and his fiancée both worked. The troops consisted of the parents, my sister, her infant son, and my brood, who were about eleven, eight, and six years old at the time. When we arrived at the hotel, it was packed. My dad scouted out my brother quickly enough and, in a few moments, what to my wondering eyes should appear but my future sister-in-law in a white, furry bunny costume, complete with ears.

She had to be miserably hot, as it was one of those costumes that has a full head and you look out through the mouth. My daughter, who was to be their flower girl that May, thought it was pretty funny. Kat was six years old at the time, and she thought she was way beyond the Easter bunny thing. She had helped dye eggs that year for the first time—why, she was practically an adult. My mom wanted to make sure the new baby could see the bunny. My nephew was only about a month old, he was completely oblivious.

My two boys were just praying no one that they knew would see them there, talking to the Easter bunny. Thankfully we didn't stay too long, and before we left, my brother in one of his usual moves gave the Easter bunny a big dramatic dip and kiss. My brother is about six foot four, so it was pretty funny to see him dip a five-foot-tall white rabbit.

As we loaded the kids up into the car, I looked over at my husband and told him that I could just hear the kids on the psychiatrist's couch now . . .

"No, really, doctor, you don't understand. My mom *is* a witch and my uncle married the Easter bunny."

Our families are important to us. We want to share our beliefs with our children and make them a part of our celebrations. The majority of us were not raised Pagan, but if your parents, siblings, and now their children are practicing Christians, you may find yourself walking a very slippery road. Religion can be a sticky subject for some families. It doesn't have to be. I am a firm believer in possessing a good sense of humor. Laugh, dammit! It's okay to look at things from the lighter side.

When our children were small, my husband and I were both concerned with the kids feeling left out of the rest of the families' holiday celebrations. In an effort to blend in, we started to celebrate double holidays twice a year, at Ostara/Easter and Yule/Christmas. The kids made out like bandits and they loved it. It also taught them to respect their grandparents' beliefs. We made the effort to teach them how their grandparents' beliefs were similar or different from our own, so that they would know. Information is always a good thing.

The biggest problem that I usually had was on Easter Sunday. That was when they traditionally show the movie *The Ten Commandments* on TV. We have Easter dinner over at the in-laws' and the TV is normally left on. My husband's family is huge, so when the kids were small I figured anything unusual they said probably would be drowned out in the roar of the crowd. Still, I knew my kids . . . so it made me nervous anyway.

Now, I happen to adore that old movie—great costumes, big sets, tons of extras, and melodramatic acting. (Yul Brynner as Rameses was such a hottie!) The problems began when my kids would get upset at the Passover scene when "they killed all the poor Egyptians."

My daughter used to cry every time. When the pharaoh lays his son's body at the temple, my middle son shouted out, "Hey, Mom! Isn't that Anubis?" My in-laws all turned to look suspiciously at me. What is a witch supposed to do? I just smiled and said, "Yes, it is." After a few moments, conversation resumed. By the Goddess, aren't kids great?

We celebrate Yule quietly at our home by lighting the Yule log and having the kids do their gift exchange with each other on that night. We make a special dinner or sometimes go out to eat. Yule has become our night for just us. It's quiet and a nice way to spend some quality time together. At our house, gifts come from Santa on the morning of the twenty-fifth.

There is no reason why a Wiccan/Pagan child can't enjoy Santa . . . who is, after all, a very magickal guy. He hangs out with elves. He has eight—count 'em, eight—magick flying reindeer. We could stretch that a bit and say he has a reindeer for every sabbat. Of course, that would play hell with the rhyming of the traditional poem "The Night Before Christmas," so . . . let's not.

There are so many different versions of Santa from around the world that it makes Santa a multicultural folk figure. Have you ever taken a good look at all the different varieties of decorative Santas that are available at stores? There are woodland Santas surrounded by animals and the English Father Christmas in a long green robe, wearing a wreath of holly. He reminds me of the Holly King. Papa Frost from Russia, attired in white, silver, and ice blue, makes a good choice. I even found a Santa that looked like Merlin all done up in celestial robes of gold and royal blue. Perfect for the solstice. You bet I bought him! Any of those characters make a great Pagan-friendly Santa, if you ask me.

Most Pagans and Wiccans have holiday wreaths, a decorated tree, and lights on their houses, and we all know where the traditional holiday decorations originated from, so why not enjoy? In all the rush and excitement of opening presents with the family, hauling your kids to Grandma's house and assorted other family homes, why worry? Just savor the season.

This rest of this chapter will be divided up into eight sections, one for each sabbat. Included are natural decorations and suggestions for relaxing sabbat celebrations for your family.

> *If Candlemas day be fair and bright,*
> *Winter will have another flight.*
> *If Candlemas day be gray and rain,*
> *Winter is gone, and will not come again.*
>
> E. HOLDEN

Candlemas/Imbolc

Candlemas is celebrated on February 1 or 2, depending on the tradition. This is the cross-quarter day between the winter solstice and the vernal (spring) equinox, and is also known as Imbolc and Brigit's or Bride's Day. Here in the States we know this as Groundhog Day. This is the day of the Virgin Maiden Goddess. The Crone has cast off her shroud and has renewed herself as the Maiden, even though winter is still holding the garden in its grip. But if you look closely, you will see signs of the garden and nature renewing itself. The days are getting longer, but some of our fiercest winter storms happen now.

Usually by this time of year I've been driving myself crazy looking at all the seed catalogs. I start to work my seed list down to a workable amount. I pacify myself by purchasing a blooming cyclamen plant or African violets. They come in handy for holiday decorations.

For household decorations, the colors of white and purple seem appropriate to me. I decorate with a few African violets or other blooming plants, and candles. Lots and lots of candles. I like to keep my Candlemas decor simple; several white candles and a blooming plant or two.

A short, sweet, and simple way to observe Brigit's Day, the sabbat of Candlemas, is to try going outdoors to watch the sunrise. Even if you are only outside for a few moments because of inclement weather, make the attempt to get outside anyway. Light a small tealight, place it in a fireproof jar or candle holder, and nestle it down into the snow. Fill up the bird food in the feeder, hang up some suet for the birds, or leave out some crusts of bread for the animals. Greet the sun as it rises and ask for Brigit's blessings. If you absolutely cannot make it outside, then light a fire in the fireplace or light a new white pillar candle and ask for Brigit's protection for your home and family. Allow the candle to burn until it goes out on its own.

Even though it is winter, get outdoors and have an outing. Celebrate nature, no matter what her season. Perhaps you could ski or go sledding. Check with your local conservation department and see what's happening with the wildlife in your neck of the woods.

In my part of the country, the bald eagles are returning to their winter home along the Mississippi and Missouri rivers. If you want a crash course in "brisk wind," try standing on the banks of the Missouri and Mississippi rivers in early February with binoculars to watch the eagles.

My family drives over to Illinois for the day, and takes a drive down the great river road. We pack a lunch, load up the crew (who really enjoy fighting over the binoculars), and off we go for the afternoon to do some eagle watching.

> *And in green underwood and cover*
> *Blossom by blossom the spring begins.*
> CHARLES ALGERNON SWINBURNE

Ostara/Spring Equinox

Ostara is a movable festival. It is celebrated on the day of the spring equinox. This usually falls around March 21. This is the festival of the Goddess Eostre. Eostre is the Norse/German goddess of the spring and the sunrise. Her symbols include the white rabbit, flowers, and, of course, colored eggs.

You could hang decorative eggs from your trees to celebrate on the morning of Ostara. I accidentally started a trend in my neighborhood by doing just that. I used to go out at sunrise on the morning of Ostara and hang a dozen pastel-colored plastic eggs from ribbons on the bottom limbs of the oak tree in the front yard. Usually, by the end of the day, many neighbors

had done the same. In the garden, the snowdrops and the crocus should be up and bloomi
by now, as well as the earlier varieties of daffodils.

Dyeing eggs with your family is one of the many pleasures of the spring equinox. The
night before the equinox, I pick up some egg dye from the grocery store (they put out holiday
stuff so early these days). Yes, I know, it blows my image not to be using natural egg dye, but
sometimes you have to be practical.

There are many recipes for natural egg dyes, some complicated and others not. One of
the best and easiest that I've found is to boil the eggs with purple cabbage leaves. After boiling
for ten to fifteen minutes, move off the heat and let the eggs sit in the pan, covered by the liquid and the leaves, overnight. In the morning the eggs will be a bright robin's egg blue. But the
color is fragile and scratches off easily, so handle them carefully.

So choose your dyes, natural or storebought. Cover the counters
with paper and turn the kids loose. At our house we
boil up a couple dozen eggs. The kids dig out a
white crayon and mark the eggs with suns, butterflies, our names, stars, and crescent moons.
They elbow each other out of the way and fight
over the purple egg dye. My three teens tease each
other unmercifully and have a great time razzing
each other about their egg-coloring skills.

On the morning of Ostara, I make cinnamon rolls to celebrate, and when the kids
were small, the bunny hid their eggs. The traditional egg hunt was completed first thing in
the morning.

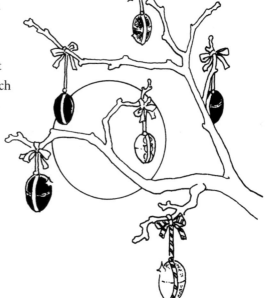

Now I serve up breakfast and hand out the presents. It amazes me just how fast a "cool" teenager reverts to childhood when faced with chocolate. "Mine!" is usually the battle cry.

Now that my kids are older I may give the boys gift certificates to a video store or jumbo packages of gum, and they all get a big candy bar. My daughter usually requests a Beanie Baby or a pair of earrings for her basket. (She still insists upon using her old purple basket.) The boys are happy with their gifts in a gift bag. It's a guy thing.

A few days before Ostara, my spring wreath goes up, along with a block set I made that spells out "Happy Ostara." This is displayed on a shelf in the living room. Check out your hometown craft store and purchase precut two-inch wooden blocks. Paint them white and then, using an alphabet stencil, choose a pastel-colored paint and stencil on the letters to spell out your message. Tip: Make your block set reversible and stencil a different greeting on the reverse side, like "Happy Beltane."

A nice spring display for your mantle or table would be decorated eggs, topiaries, ceramic white rabbits, bird's nests, and fresh flowers. Clip some daffodils and tulips from your yard, put them in an old canning jar or vase, and work in some twigs of blooming forsythia or pussy willow for a casual homemade arrangement. Try lining an old stoneware or wooden bowl with moss and fill it up with artificial eggs. Save the eggs and reuse them every year.

Check out the florist or garden center for pansies and violas, you can plant these now. I love pansies in containers and window boxes. Pansies will tolerate most cold weather, though if the cold swings back into extreme temperatures, you may have to cover them up for a night or two.

Also at this time of year, hyacinths, tulips, and daffodils in gift containers become available. Blooming bulbs in baskets or wrapped pots would make a nice centerpiece for your table. And you can jazz it up a little. Cover the soil with sheet moss and then tuck some pastel eggs into the moss for a delightful display. Happy spring!

O'Brignal banks are wild and fair
And Greeta woods are green,
And you may gather garlands there
Would grace a summer queen.

SIR WALTER SCOTT

May Day/Beltane

As I write this, it is Beltane day, May 1. The mantle is decorated with moss-covered topiaries, a bird's nest, and birdhouses. The wood-burning stove has been cleaned out for the summer, and my big old cauldron is on the hearth, filled with a trailing ivy.

By Beltane the garden is really greening up, and the early blooming plants—such as lily of the valley, bleeding hearts, and columbine—are blooming prettily. The hostas are filling in and the astilbe are beginning to show color. The ferns are thickening up and growing taller. The two new hanging baskets that I planted last week are starting to fill in more, the snaps are taller, and the allysum is fuller. The pink and dark purple petunias are blooming well now, and smell terrific after sundown. My climbing roses, of the variety *Zephrine Drouhin*, are setting blooms, and in about two weeks they will put on a traffic-stopping performance in cerise pink.

The pansies that I planted in March are really luxurious now. The peonies are showing color, and I find myself checking the garden to see how many plants need to be transplanted or thinned out. My husband is in his search-for-the-most-interesting-heirloom-tomato mode, and I can't seem to make it past a flower stand or nursery without stopping, for just a quick peek.

Ah, May. The time of year when the bugs aren't too bad and you can enjoy a evening outdoors without the bug spray. Here in Missouri, it is now safe to plant those tender annuals like impatiens, begonias, and petunias. I find myself looking forward to the full moon in May; we call it the faery moon at my house. This is the night when I bless the garden and all of the herbs, flowers, plants, trees, and vegetables we care for in our yard. Both Beltane and the faery moon are magickal times for gardens and gardening.

Beltane is a fertility festival. Opposite on the wheel of the year from Samhain, it is an in-between time. The boundaries between our world and the other realms are thinnest at Samhain and Beltane. For those who wish to commune with the faery realms, Beltane would be the time to try. Refer to chapter 7 for more faery information, and be careful! You just might get what you ask for.

The maypole is a customary symbol of this day, as well as bright, ice-cream colors for its ribbons or, if you prefer, the more traditional red and white. May baskets hung on doors, stuffed full of flowers, are customary decorations, as well as flower garlands woven for the hair. Check those floral languages and leave someone an enchanted message bouquet.

At my house, if the weather cooperates, we have a barbeque and eat our dinner outside. I usually serve strawberry shortcake for dessert.

Later, after the kids go to bed and I have some alone time, I head outside to the garden for a chance to be alone with the Lord and Lady to thank them for their blessings and maybe, just maybe, to catch a glimpse of the faeries.

A noise like of a hidden brook
In the leafy month of June,
That to the sleeping woods all night
Singeth a quiet tune.

SAMUEL TAYLOR COLERIDGE

Midsummer/Summer Solstice

Midsummer or the summer solstice is on or around June 21, the longest day of the year and the shortest night. Decorating ideas are seashells and starfish arranged across your altar or mantle. You could really be subtle and go Americana—use architectural stars and folk art in country colors of blues and reds.

Midsummer is celebrated at my house by barbequing, going to the pool, camping, or the occasional fishing trip. Some other ideas for celebrating the solstice are midsummer garden parties, going on a picnic, or taking a trip to the lake or beach.

To create an inexpensive midsummer garden party, keep the menu fresh and light. Decorate a picnic table if you have one, or drag your kitchen table out to the garden. Use a tablecloth in any pretty pastel shade and either use floral theme paper plates or your good dishes. I like to mix and match glassware and plates for a more informal look. You might try picking up some plastic tumblers in bright shades of hot summer colors.

How about creating individual tussie-mussies for your guests or, better yet, have everyone make their own while they are at the party? Put a pretty book on the table explaining the symbolism of the flowers, set out some supplies and flowers, and turn them loose.

If you are having your magickal friends over, try a solstice/celestial theme: gold suns with blue and gold plates and napkins. Sprinkle some glittery stars and moon confetti on the tablecloth. If children are invited, you could make it a faery party. Let the little ones dress up as

faeries—the adults, too, if they wish. Embellish place cards with glitter pens and floral, faery, or celestial stickers, depending on your theme.

Snip some blooming roses off your bushes and use garden flowers and blooming fragrant herbs for a centerpiece. For faery lights you can use old glass canning jars with a tealight inside and set them in a row down the center of the table or place them throughout the garden. After the sun goes down, light up some sparklers for the kids and the adults. Have an enchanted midsummer's night!

Summer afternoon—summer afternoon;
to me those have always been the two most
beautiful words in the English language.

HENRY JAMES

Lughnasadh/Lammas

Lughnasadh is the first of three harvest festivals, and baking bread is traditional. However, I use a bread machine. I love those things! If time is an issue, you could make cornbread. Pick up a mix at the store and whip it together. My kids like to make cornbread, it doesn't take any longer than a few minutes to mix it up and pop it into the oven. Serve it with butter, honey, or maple syrup.

Decorate your home and altar with sunflowers, gourds, wheat, and scarecrows. Make a basket centerpiece with gourds and ornamental corn. Use a flat-bottom basket and arrange the gourds and corn around a central yellow or orange pillar candle.

In the garden, the Indian corn is ready to be harvested and the tomatoes are putting out lots of fruit. This is the time of year I start to get a little anxious over the pumpkin crop. How are they doing? Will we have a good crop this year?

Blackberries are ripening and if time permits I make the drive with my sister-in-law to her husband's family property to go blackberry picking. The kids are getting ready to go back to school in a few weeks, and mothers everywhere are counting down the days. I usually perform a little abundance/prosperity work at this time of year, in thanks for the harvest from the garden and to help me stretch the budget in our annual "time to buy school clothes" season.

On the day of Lughnasadh/Lammas, August 1, fix a tealight inside of a small cauldron. Place around the outside of the cauldron an arrangement of fruits and vegetables from the

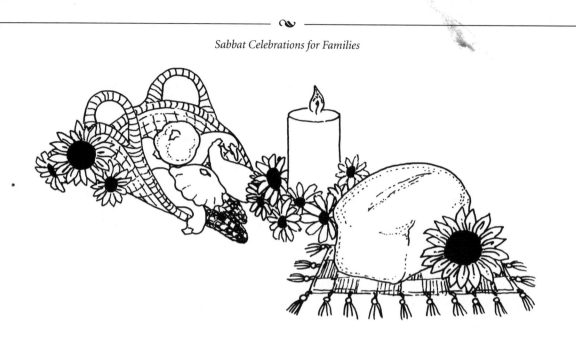

garden. Suggested garden items would be decorative Indian corn, gourds, garden tomatoes, peppers, eggplants, a dish of blackberries set to the side or a ring of different-colored apples from the market. These would be nice if your garden isn't producing anything edible at the moment. Use whatever strikes your fancy—be imaginative, you'll come up with something clever. As you light the candle, ask for continued blessings for your family in your own words, or try something like this:

> *Welcome, the season of the first harvest*
>
> *Your continued blessings I now request.*
>
> *We give thanks for the gifts bestowed upon us*
>
> *May our family prosper and enjoy success.*

Let the candle burn out and then cook up the fruit and vegetables however you prefer for Lughnasadh dinner.

There is nothing in the world more peaceful
than apple leaves with an early moon.

ALICE MEYNELL

Mabon/Autumnal Equinox

Also known as the Witches' Thanksgiving. Our menu consists of a turkey dinner, all the trimmings, and pumpkin and apple pie for dessert. Seasonal decorations include fall leaves, a cornucopia, pumpkins, and apples. In the garden I am watching the pumpkin crop and starting to harvest them. The pumpkins get lined up on wooden planks in the backyard until the end of the month, when the kids will start to sell them. Fall mums are everywhere and I pump up the color in the autumn garden by picking up a few mums and planting them in spots that could use a dash of color. A garland of fall leaves intertwined with orange lights is draped over the outside front door.

On Mabon we put up our corn stalks in the front yard. Six-Foot Stanley comes out of the attic and is displayed in the front yard gardens. Stanley is a scarecrow that my husband rigged up on a two-by-four frame and dressed in some old jeans and a shirt, many years ago. I added a bandanna and hat. Ken then painted an "Autumn Greetings" sign to be placed by Stanley's side. Stanley stays with us, watching over the yard, until after Samhain/Halloween.

Stanley stands about six feet tall and his head is one of those realistic-looking, light-up, carved jack-o'-lanterns that is bolted onto the frame. We place an old fishing hat on his head and put the jack-o'-lantern light on a timer so when the sun goes down his head lights up. The neighborhood children love Stanley. He seems to have his own fan club. In late September and throughout October, carloads of families go by, waving and shouting hello to Stanley. He seems to have started a decorating trend of his own as well. After Stanley makes his Mabon appearance, other variations of Stanley, sitting on benches and sprawled in yards, start to appear in the neighborhood front yards by the very next day.

One family tradition that I insist on is going apple picking on Mabon. Depending on my son's football games and our work schedules, we try to go on the actual day of the equinox, or as close as we can get. I take my family out to the same farm that my parents took me to. They give you a tractor ride out to the orchard and turn you loose. There is nothing like eating an apple as soon as you pick it off the tree!

Someone always starts an apple fight by throwing fallen apples at somebody else (the culprit is usually my husband). I snap lots of pictures of the kids who, of course, roll their eyes at me and tell me they're too old to have their pictures taken. I start by asking nicely. Then I get tougher and start barking orders—"You stand there . . . You, quit smacking your sister . . . You, take off your sunglasses . . . Come on, guys, *smile*. Act like you like each other!"—and finally, they give in. I wouldn't trade that family outing for anything.

Listen! The wind is rising and
the air is wild with leaves.
We have had our summer evenings,
now for October eves!

HUMBERT WOLFE

Halloween/Samhain

The serious Halloween decorations go out October 1. I have more Halloween accessories than some folks have Christmas decorations. No kidding. I have a collection of folk-art style, kitchen-witch dolls that stays displayed on shelves in the kitchen year 'round. With the dolls are a couple of framed Victorian-style Halloween postcards. I collect anything clever that has a Halloween theme on it, or an attractive representation of a witch. No green-faced hags! In this small collection of mine there are dolls, tins, mugs, a teapot, and my own witchy needlework.

Every room in the house, except for the bathrooms, gets decorated with a little something. I usually can talk one of my sons into hanging up my orange Halloween lights across the front of the house. A spinoff of those white winter icicle lights, these lights are orange icicle types that some enterprising soul named Witch-cicles. I found them on sale. Who could resist? Certainly not me. Besides, they look terrific as a backdrop for Stanley. It is about this time of year that we can hear carloads of families with kids who have been admiring Stanley shouting, "That house! I wanna go to that house!" as they drive by. Even my "cool" teens smile and get a kick out of that.

About a week before Samhain, I put up spiderwebs and set out a couple of hay bales to display all the pumpkins on. I might, if I can find some on sale, buy a few bright red or orange mums for the front porch and place them in pots, just for decoration. That's my Martha Stewart side coming out again. Can't help it, it's a sickness.

As a family, we argue over which pumpkin carving patterns to buy that year, and then the race is on to claim a pattern and find the perfect pumpkin to fit it. Some patterns we save and reuse from year to year. As you can imagine, we carve up around a dozen pumpkins or so. On Halloween night, the kids arrange them by lining them up on hay bales and along the garden sidewalk. They look pretty impressive from the street.

Owing to all the decorations that are clever, spirited, and attractive—not gross or scary—we get many trick-or-treaters every year. It is always amusing to hear the parents as their kids drag them up the sidewalk on Halloween night. Many parents walk up to the porch and ask where we got all the pumpkins, and how did we carve them up so neatly? Most have told me how their kids have been hounding them for weeks to come to our house. I have come to be known in the neighborhood as the "lady with all the pumpkins on the corner." Believe it or not, I get asked many gardening questions on that night. While the trick-or-treaters check out the pumpkins, their parents usually check out the front garden.

A interesting way to make a seasonal arrangement for your Samhain table is to hollow out a medium-sized pumpkin. Insert a block of florist's foam called Oasis. Presoak the Oasis in water overnight, then trim to size and slip into the pumpkin shell. Leave about a half an inch of the foam sticking above the opening of your pumpkin. Cover the exposed foam with moss, and secure with a few floral pins.

Clip blooming mums, sedum, roses, cosmos, and whatever other flowers your fall garden is producing, and make a simple round arrangement in the pumpkin. If you don't want to mess with the foam, try hiding an old clean jar inside the pumpkin. Then fill the jar with water and arrange your flowers inside of that.

Another fun idea is to clean out mini pumpkins or small round gourds and carve primitive or folk-art style little stars and crescent moons on their sides. Place a tealight inside of the mini pumpkins and then arrange them down your buffet table and light them up. These tiny pumpkin luminaries are also quite dramatic and different when placed on a candelabra instead of bigger candles.

When my crew of ghouls and goblins were smaller, we started putting out a buffet of finger foods and sandwiches to get them to eat dinner and to keep them from devouring all of their candy. The menu habitually includes rye bread and dill dip, carrots, celery, chicken salad sandwiches on rolls, and assorted cheese and crackers, dips and chips. For dessert, a pumpkin pie. When our nieces and nephews arrive that night they often find their way to the buffet table for a snack.

Now that my kids are older and only one of them is trick-or-treating, they still enjoy the buffet. It amuses me to have them haul out the Halloween tablecloth and argue with me over the menu and which centerpiece to use on the table. Another family tradition is to watch the movie *Young Frankenstein* together on Halloween. Each of us knows all the lines by heart.

After the trick-or-treaters are gone and my kids stagger off to bed, I head outside for a private Samhain celebration. I leave a candle lit for the spirits of the dead to burn all night in the big iron cauldron in the living room. I take a few moments to honor the souls of those who have passed away that year. Then I welcome the season of winter, reflect on that year's growing season, and start to anticipate my time of rest from the hard work of gardening.

> *The holly and the ivy*
> *When they are both full grown,*
> *Of all the trees that are in the wood,*
> *The holly bears the crown.*
>
> TRADITIONAL CAROL

Yule/Winter Solstice

The winter solstice or Yule is both the longest night and the shortest day. From this point on, the sun becomes stronger and stronger and the daylight hours begin to slowly increase. The birth of the newborn sun is celebrated, as well as the official beginning of winter. Yule logs decorated with fresh pine, sprigs of holly, and red taper candles are traditional Pagan accessories. So are large, red, cinnamon-scented "sun" candles.

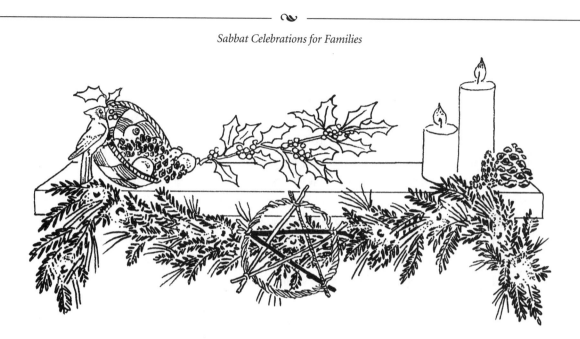

Speaking of candles, those pillars are on sale during late November and December, so go snag some for your seasonal candle magick. Dark green pillars with the familiar scents of pine and bayberry add their own magickal aromatherapy to the home; pine for abundance and protection, the scent of bayberry for bringing good luck in the new year, the fragrance of cinnamon for love and prosperity, and off-white candles in vanilla scents to soothe the nerves and encourage loving vibrations.

For a natural, rustic-looking arrangement for your holiday altar or mantle, try either live or artificial pine swags with white lights sprinkled throughout. Add red, off-white, and green pillar candles in various heights and group them together on either end of the altar/mantle. Create some rustic twig pentagrams by cutting fallen twigs into twelve-inch sections and then binding the ends together with wire. Tuck those into your display.

For your Yule tree, look for outdoor theme ornaments. Hunting and fishing ornaments, bears, birds, small reindeer, a silk cardinal for a tree topper. Fill in with decorative bird's nests and lots of bright red berries and pine cones to finish up your woodland Yule decorations.

For a solstice or celestial theme, decorate with golds and blues, and gilded ornaments in the shape of suns, stars, and moons. Watch for Pagan-friendly ornaments like a stag or oak leaves, and add as many sun ornaments as you can find. White lights, crystal-looking icicles, and snowflakes will add a wintery sparkle. Try looping iridescent ribbon through your greenery on the mantle and group together gold, white, and a few red pillar candles.

My last suggestion is inspired by a miniature tree that I redecorated a few years ago. This small tabletop tree looked like a Charlie Brown tree. It sat on a table at the end of the hall and was pretty sad-looking. All the odds and ends over the years were thrown on it. One day the floral designer in me snuck out and I pulled everything but the white lights off that little tree and took a critical look at it. I had three very nice ornaments with angels and Santas on them—these were the old-fashioned, card-type ornaments that are heavy cardboard with gold edges and have reproduction Victorian-looking designs on them. There were two angels that looked like faeries and one Santa. All the ornaments were in shades of mauve, white, and gold.

With visions of flower faeries and sugarplums dancing through my head, I went to the craft store and hunted through their sale holiday floral picks. I found roses dusted in glitter in shades of mauve and deep pink. I dug deeper and found some grape clusters and tiny apples in coordinating shades, also dusted in that sugary-looking glitter.

In a half-price bin, my husband unearthed a set of a dozen tiny glass ball ornaments. They were mauve, frosted white, and celadon green. We discovered a tiny tree topper star in glittery white and I bought a spool of sale ribbon in sheer white with gold wire edges. We added some mushroom birds in pink and a butterfly to that little tree, and created a knockout miniature garden faery/sugarplum tree. The whole project cost me about ten dollars.

The three trees described for you are all theme trees that we have in our home. The solstice/celestial tree is the only big tree, however. The woodland tree is a four-foot tree for the family room. The faery tree is a tabletop tree and it is about two feet tall.

Before you toss up your hands in disgust at the decorating maniac in me, I want to tell you that all of the decorations I have described have taken me years to build up slowly. I watch for sales and make what I can't afford to buy.

Do I have any projects left? Oh, yeah, I have to redo my artificial pine wreath for the front door, it's looking a little worse for wear. I have a great big three-dimensional sun ornament that hangs in the middle of the holiday wreath and I want to incorporate that in somehow, maybe add some glittery fruit or golden pears . . . I'm not exactly sure what I'll do with it. But I promise you, I'll come up with something.

10

Everybody needs places to play in and pray in,
where nature may heal and cheer
and give strength . . .
JOHN MUIR

Garden Magick from the Ground Up

What, do you suppose, turns a typical flower garden into an enchanted garden? What elements do you imagine would have to be incorporated to transform an outdoor area, such as the typical backyard, into a sacred space? Think about this for a moment. You could work with the four basic elements of natural magick, earth, air, fire, and water. Incorporating those into your sacred space would be a fantastic way to start. Are any other ideas coming to mind? Yes, there are various statues and representations of the God and Goddess available. Those could make nifty, magickal garden decorations. I can just imagine the little wheels in your mind busily turning away . . .

However, before you start thinking too much in terms of garden accessories and knick-knacks, hang on for a minute. I wasn't speaking of something corporeal that you'll have to go out and purchase. No, I was thinking like a witch. I was envisioning more along the lines of the metaphysical and the spiritual. Now I've intrigued you, haven't I?

The single most important and powerful aspect of turning the mundane yard into the magickal sanctuary would be *you*. Yes, you. You and your magickal will and intentions. In truth, the difference between the magickal and the mundane garden is the deliberate act of consecrating the area for the purpose of creating a permanent sacred space. This sacred garden space would be both an area in which to raise your enchanted plants and a place to perform magick. If we are to enter into the world of herbal enchantments and garden magick, we need to leave our excuses and preconceptions behind. It is time to step up and go to work. The easiest way to accomplish this is to get off your rump and start to work in the garden.

Now is the moment to get your hands dirty. You need to begin to put what you've learned about flower folklore and magickal herbalism into practice. Let's make it a part of your everyday life. As you work within the traditions of garden witchery, the garden becomes a place where both our metaphysical and ordinary lives begin to thrive together.

Sweet is the lore which Nature brings.
WORDSWORTH
∿

Nature, the Ultimate Sacred Space

In chapter 2 we talked briefly about creating your own outdoor sanctuary. Let's expand on that a bit. Find a relaxing, private place outside, a natural sacred space for you to perform your herbal spells and to garden. Go outside right now, and scout out a likely spot, someplace private that feels right to you. You will know it when you've found it. You may get a bit of a tingle or even a rush. Some folks get a sense of peace, and they'll notice more activity from birds and insects, like butterflies or bees for example.

At home, my sacred garden space is the entire side yard. The side yard is surrounded by a six-foot privacy fence and shielded at one end by large maple trees. This area incorporates the back patio, shade gardens, the rose arbor, and a small fountain. At the other end of the side yard is a full sun exposure area. This flower bed runs along the entire length of our house.

In this sunny bed, I have roses and many of my magickal "sunny" herbs growing all crammed in together, cottage style, such as lamb's ears, tall Russian sage, rue, several varieties of yarrow, coneflowers, phlox, feverfew, and balloon flowers. A pink clematis, growing up the corner section of the privacy fence, frames the garden gate and then peeks over the top of the fence.

Even though we have gardens that surround the house, it is here in my "working space" that guests are always drawn to. With all of the magickal work that I and my family have done in the garden over the years, it definitely carries a mystical energy all of its own.

I want to point out that your personal sacred space does not have to take up an entire section of your yard. I have magickal friends who use their front porches or apartment decks as their outdoor sacred space. They arrange hanging baskets, containers, and pots of magickal herbs and flowers about their porch or deck. Then they add accessories like a little table and a comfortable lawn chair.

My friend Amy uses a cushioned wicker love seat and a matching small coffee table to set a candle and her other magickal supplies onto. Her little back deck is her personal sacred space. She loves it out there. Some nights after her two kids go to bed, she grabs a glass of wine, heads out to the deck, and sits there in solitary splendor, reading, relaxing, or performing her magick.

Large or small, the size of your personal sacred garden space does not matter. You do not require an elaborate setup. Go with what you have. I may have a large sacred space in the side yard, but I usually choose a specific small spot for my spellcasting. When the roses bloom in May, I sit under the rose arbor. During the hot summer months, I work in the shade garden. On nights of the full moon, I stand in the middle of my "full sun exposure" flower beds and cast my spells. No one can see me out there. I am hidden behind the privacy fence, and this particular garden faces southeast and gives me an unrestricted view of the rising moon. Sometimes I simply sit in the grass in the middle of the garden and drag a small table over next to me, to set a candle or two on.

Some garden witches might set up at the backyard picnic table and keep an eye on their little ones while they run around the yard. You could toss down a blanket and sit on the ground, next to a favorite blooming shrub. Or perform your magick quietly under a tree. Again, it is how it feels to you that is the important thing. Ideally, you want to be comfortably surrounded by nature. On the porch, deck, or in the backyard, garden witches adapt to their environment and go where the magick of nature leads them.

Setting Up Your Sacred Space

To set up your sacred space, mark your four cardinal directions or points. If you need to use a compass, then do so. Otherwise put your back to the rising sun one morning and hold your arms straight out to your sides. You will look like a human letter *T*. Here is how you mark out your cardinal points. Your back is meeting the east. Your left arm is the south. Your nose points the way to the west, and your right arm is facing the north. Get it? You could make yourself a set of permanent garden markers to help you remember where the directions are. Try using small decorative rocks or polished stones.

You may mark each cardinal point with the stone or some other type of natural garden accent. Try painting four smooth stones to use as quarter markers. Paint one green for the element of earth and the direction north; yellow for the element of air and the east; red for fire and the south; and lastly, blue for the element of water and the direction west. Then place these markers in the appropriate spots to designate your sacred space.

Don't like the idea of using a rock as a marker? How about a separate container garden to mark each of the four quarters instead? Here's an idea . . . all red flowers, like salvia or cockscomb, grown in a container for the southern quarter. This would represent the element of fire beautifully. The flame-shaped blossoms and the hot color would be complementary to this quarter's energies.

Other colors of plants and flowers that you could incorporate might be earthy green foliage and ferns for the north. Blues and purples for the watery west, and airy and soft yellow and white flowers for the east. What other kinds of flowers or herbs do you imagine you could use?

As long as we are discussing the four quarters and the elements, let's add a natural representation for each of the four elements as well. This will enhance your garden and your natural magick, as it will help you to link more closely into each of the four magickal elements.

For earth, you could incorporate stones and crystals. To acknowledge the element of air, you could set out a few fallen feathers that you have collected. To announce and celebrate the breeze as it blows through your garden, hang up a set of wind chimes, or you could place a bird feeder in the eastern quarter. For the element of fire, try garden lanterns or candles, or perhaps some decorative garden lighting. Finally, the element of water could be represented by a small fountain or a water feature, such as a bird bath or even a small saucer filled with water for the birds to drink from. Encourage the birds, squirrels, and beneficial insects to live in your garden. Make it a happy and safe haven for them and for you.

Now that you have your sacred space all set up (or at least planned out), we should supply you with some spells and charms for this occasion. This elemental trio of charms is to be used to designate your new sacred garden space and to bless your magickal garden and plants. Note: If you prefer, you may also use the "Faery Blessing" charm from chapter 7.

Blessings for the Garden

Announcing Sacred Space

I call the Spirits of Nature, the Great Mother and Father.

Assist me now, by the powers of earth, air, fire, and water.

Merge your magick with mine, circle around this place,

As we now announce the creation of a sacred garden space.

Blessing of the Elements

Come water, earth, fire, and wind,

To me, your sacred powers lend.

This garden of mine is now sacred space,

By the elements four, I bless this place.

A Garden Blessing

Through the seasons of rain, sun, and snow,

May these plants and herbs happily grow.

Winter to spring and summer to fall,

Lord and Lady, bless them one and all.

The things that all sacred garden spaces have in common are they are outside, so magickal herbs and plants are close at hand. The sacred space has a working area—a place to sit and a small table or safe surface to work on. The four elements are somehow represented. And finally, the sacred space is consecrated, blessed, and relatively private.

Even if it may be bare bones in your yard right now, don't be discouraged. It's okay, you have plenty of time and opportunity to build that garden. Instead, think of the possibilities! Come up with a plan. Decide what you can do yourself to improve your landscape and future magickal garden over the next few years. Start small, with an eye on expanding the garden's boundaries outward later on.

> *. . . with silver bells and cockle shells*
> *and pretty maids all in a row.*
> MOTHER GOOSE

How Does Your Magick Garden Grow?

I want to make very clear to you that my gardens did not just *poof!* appear suddenly overnight. It took several years to accomplish what we have today. The gardens are always evolving and changing. Gardeners, both magickal and mundane, are forever learning and trying something new in the yard. My family and I transplant or thin out some perennials every spring and we move things around occasionally. I like to try new plant varieties from time to time. Show me a gardener who doesn't.

Does everything I plant turn out splendidly? No, not always. I make mistakes too. Sometimes you pat yourself on the back, amazed at your own cleverness, and now and then you make a bad plant choice and then you ruthlessly pull things out.

For example, I ripped out most of my side yard's sunny bed two years ago this spring, as it had been overtaken by evening primrose. Evening primrose is a lovely perennial that makes lots of pink blooms and tolerates poor soils. It is, however, extremely aggressive and can overtake a bed in a few years. In my case they were starting to choke out some of my other magickal perennials.

So, faced with an all-out perennial war, I checked the almanac and timed my transplanting down with a waning moon. We dug out all but my biggest perennials and set them in the shade. Then I had my oldest son go through the bed and around the big perennials with a rototiller. My neighbors thought I was crazy, ripping into the garden that way. But it needed it. We raked and pulled out all of the offending primrose. I then amended the soil with compost and humus. My husband, son, and I divided up the phlox, yarrow, and coneflowers and transplanted these and my other perennials back into the improved bed all in the same day. To finish, we watered them in well by hand. (I didn't want a sprinkler to beat them all down.) Later that evening, I went outside and checked on the newly transplanted plants. A few needed more water. So I gave them all a drink again and blessed the garden so our plants would thrive.

I was rewarded with a happy, healthy cottage garden that year. The following summer the coneflowers grew heartily and the purple garden phlox grew five feet tall. No kidding. I have pictures of my daughter standing next to the phlox. They are almost as tall as she is. During the months of June and July, as the phlox bloomed, the garden was fabulously scented. It was especially fragrant at night and it looked and felt like a faery tale out there. Amazing what a little hard work combined with magick can accomplish, isn't it?

I have caught hold of the earth,
to use a gardener's phrase,
and neither friends nor my enemies
will find it an easy matter
to transplant me again.

HENRY ST. JOHN, LORD BOLINGBROKE

◯∿

Digging In

Wow, we really have dug in good, haven't we? Let's see. . . we talked about turning back into the rhythms and tides of nature. We went over mystic plants and trees, and discovered that magickal herbs and plants are to be found everywhere and are easy for the average home-owner to grow. We used our time constructively while looking at astrological timing and gardening by the moon. We greeted the Goddess and reviewed deities that correspond to nature, the moon signs, and phases for gardening. We delved into antique flower folklore and talked about the joys and risks of working with nature spirits and the faeries. We covered ideas for garden witch crafts and creating a garden witch's BOS. We even went over suggestions for natural family sabbat celebrations. Finally, we plotted and planned out ideas for creating and consecrating outdoor magickal gardens and sacred spaces.

Well, what could possibly be left? Only the toughest part of your training: committing some basic herbal knowledge to memory. Transplanting your new herbal knowledge into your spellwork. And, finally, creating your own garden witch spells and rhymes.

Strange to the world, he wore a bashful look,
The fields his study, Nature was his book.

ROBERT BLOOMFIELD

~

Hitting the Books

It's time to hit the books. Visit the library and start reading up on the topics of perennials, general gardening, and herbs. It is very much worth your time. Watch the clearance tables at the larger bookstores. Occasionally you will find a great bargain on a gardening book or two. Talk to other gardeners, and see which books are their favorites. A few good reference books are vital for any research. A handful of the books that I would recommend for your herbal and magickal reference shelf are as follows:

Herbs by Lesley Bremness (DK Books, 2000).

Cunningham's Encyclopedia of Magical Herbs by Scott Cunningham
(Llewellyn, 1985).

Cunningham's Encyclopedia of Crystal and Gem Magic by Scott Cunningham
(Llewellyn, 1992).

Magical Herbalism: The Secret Craft of the Wise by Scott Cunningham
(Llewellyn, 1982).

The Women's Dictionary of Symbols and Sacred Objects by Barbra Walker
(Castle Books, 1988).

An ABC of Witchcraft Past and Present by Doreen Valiente (Phoenix Publishing, 1973).
This is an excellent all-around reference book.

The Witches' Way by Janet and Stewart Farrar (Phoenix Publishing, 1984). A definite, thoroughly British classic.

Moon Magick by D. J. Conway (Llewellyn, 1995). If you are stumped for ideas or just want information and suggestions for specific deities, this is a fabulous book and one of my all-around favorites.

Take a good look at these books. Now, have you ever noticed that most modern Pagan/Wiccan authors have books by Scott Cunningham, Doreen Valiente, and the Farrars in their bibliographies? Think there might be a reason for that? If you have a modern magickal book that has really helped you or is one of your favorites, check that book's bibliography. Then go track down those books. Dust off your library card and start researching. Think of it as a sort of quest, and it is. It's a quest for knowledge.

It is so easy to whimper and whine about a lack of advanced material, and so much harder to experiment and create your own. It will take time and effort and, besides, you need something to keep you busy on rainy days and during the long winter months anyway. (Don't even tell me that you don't know how.) Basic correspondence charts are everywhere. Refer to them until you get the rudiments of magick memorized.

The resourceful garden witch is one that carefully researches various magickal traditions and pantheons and knows their basic magickal and herbal correspondences. That way they can quickly and easily design and cast spells of their own creation. The finest quarter calls, herbal spells, and flower charms are truly the ones that you invent yourself.

To create a little flower is the labor of ages.

WILLIAM BLAKE

Creating Your Own Style of Garden Witchery

To rhyme or not to rhyme, that is the question. If you have trouble making your herbal charms and spells rhyme (and you don't have a thirteen-year-old rhyming wizard living with you), go get yourself a rhyming dictionary. Keep your charms short, sweet, and uncomplicated. Don't worry about trying to sound like Byron or Yeats. I like to think of the formula for creating spells that rhyme in a very elementary way—that old den mother adage of KISMIF, which stands for *Keep It Simple, Make It Fun.*

At first, teaching myself to write herbal spells that rhymed made my stomach tie itself up into a knot. Who was I kidding? I'm not a poet. I made myself a nervous wreck trying to sound fluid and elegant. Then I realized I'm neither of those things. What I am is no-nonsense, slightly sarcastic, and funny. No matter how serious I try to be, the humor always sneaks back out. So I just made the charms and spells sound like me. That took the pressure off, and I began to enjoy the process. And, wonder of wonders, that turned the trick.

Use your imagination. I've completely lost count of how many times I have suggested that to you. Look for inspiration everywhere, especially in nature. You may find yourself moved to create new quarter calls or spells in the most unusual places . . .

While I was traipsing through the woods, vainly trying to keep up with my trout-fishing family this past summer, I was inspired to write a new set of quarter calls. At the time, I was finishing up the first draft of this book and realized that with all of my talk of herbal spells and charms, I had yet to include any circle castings. (How remiss of me.) I had the idea, rolling around in my head, to possibly write a circle casting that incorporated magickal flowers or herbs.

Now, as you know, a complete quarter call generally includes a salute to each individual direction, a call to the coordinating element, and an invocation of that element's specific qualities, such as west, water, love . . . following me so far?

As I tagged along behind the family, admiring the wildflowers along the stream bank, I stopped to appreciate a gorgeous wild hydrangea in bloom. I then noticed a tough little cypress tree growing close by. He was next to a huge oak and then surrounded by lots of young oak trees, all growing in a circle. That got me to thinking . . . what about a circle call working with the magick of trees instead?

As we hiked back to the cabin for lunch, I looked around at the various trees, growing wild in the park. After the meal, I sent the troops back out and I settled down alone with a note pad and wrote the following.

This quarter call does indeed draw on trees and their magickal attributes. You will notice that there are coordinating times of day as well as directions and magickal correspondences. To perform this circle casting, start in the east. As you call each quarter, you will keep moving to each new direction to your right. Then move to the center to seal the circle.

CIRCLE OF THE TREES

In the east, maple leaves rustle in the morning breeze,

Element of air, I call for inspiration, join me now, please.

In the south, the midday sun shines upon the mighty oak tree,

I request the element of fire for strength and to illuminate me.

In the west, the willow sways by the silver springs at twilight,

Element of water, I call for love and the gift of second sight.

In the north grows the cypress, tree of the midnight hour,

Element of earth, grant me protection, wisdom, and power.

Four different trees of magick, four separate times of power.

This circle of trees is now cast by root, stem, leaf, and flower.

To open this circle, begin in the north. Release each element with your love and thanks. Try something like this:

Element of the earth, I thank you for your presence. Go in peace. Blessed be.

Then move to your left and release each element in turn—west, then the south, and finally the east. To finish up, I would open the circle by using that oldie but goodie Craft standard, "The circle is open, but unbroken. Merry meet, merry part, and merry meet again."

> *There's rosemary, that's for remembrance;*
> *pray, love, remember: and there is pansies,*
> *that's for thoughts.*
>
> SHAKESPEARE, *HAMLET*

Writing Your Own Herbal Spells and Charms

How do you begin writing your own herbal spells, you may wonder? Remember all of those correspondence charts found in the other chapters of this book? There were charts for astrological associations, color magick, crystals, goddess correlations, floral languages, and magickal plants. Refer to those. They should be able to get you rolling.

When I first began to create my own garden witchery spells, I usually wrote everything out on paper. That way, I could work all the bugs out and it helped me to identify and then use colors, crystals, flowers, plants, and herbs that worked in sympathy with one another. Here is a spell worksheet for you to refer to and then work from.

Garden Witch Spell Worksheet

Goal: _____

Day: _____

Moon phase: _____

Moon sign: _____

Deity invoked: _____

Herbs used and their magickal application: _____

_____

Flowers used and their magickal significance: _____

_____

Candle color (if you would incorporate candle magick): _____

Crystals or stones: _____

Charm or verse: _____

_____

Setup (equipment, such as candle holders, a vase, a cauldron, or fireproof bowl): _____

_____

Results (how long it took for this spell to work, and any results that you noticed): _____

_____

_____

_____

Let's give you a hands-on type of example of how to pull this all together. Imagine that you're sitting at home, sick with a nasty sinus infection. (This requires no effort for me at the moment as I have one myself—and to top it off, I have also completely lost my voice.) After calling the doctor and getting them to send out some antibiotics two days ago, I am slowly recovering. However, it's back to work for me tomorrow, and I still feel pretty wobbly. So I decide to take matters into my own hands and work a little healing magick for myself.

Okay then, what flowers or herbs do I have available to me at the moment? It is late November and, as I look out the window, I notice that a rose bush of mine is still blooming. It is a red and white rose called Love. That will work out fine, as red and white are both goddess colors. Rose petals are used magickally to "speed things up," so I can work with that to speed my recovery. White is an all-purpose color in magick, and the color red is often incorporated into healing rituals.

I toss on my coat, slip on my shoes, and head outside with a pair of pruners. What else is available to me out here? There was a bit of ice in the rain that fell yesterday. The garden is chilly, sparkling, and it looks downright magickal. Little drops of ice are dangling from the branches and plants. I am amazed that this rosebud looks so healthy. As I walk quickly around the gardens, I pluck some catnip, a leaf or two of the green ferny-looking yarrow foliage, and a bit of rue.

Back inside, I tuck all but the catnip into a vase and sit down to assemble the components for the rest of my herbal spell. I gave the catnip to the kitties—they smelled it on me a soon as I walked in the back door.

My notes might look something like this . . .

GOAL: To recover from this sinus infection.

DAY: Thursday, a Jupiter day. Jupiter days can be used for health and good luck. (See chapter 6.)

MOON PHASE: Waxing, it becomes a full moon tomorrow. To augment the recovery process. Full moon energies for extra power.

MOON SIGN: Taurus, an earth day. That's handy, we are doing earthy magick, after all.

DEITY INVOKED: The Mother Goddess.

HERBS USED AND THEIR MAGICKAL APPLICATIONS: Rue helps you recover from an illness. Yarrow is a witch's herb, it's all purpose.

FLOWERS USED AND THEIR MAGICKAL SIGNIFICANCE: A red and white petaled rose to speed things up and to promote peace and love. (Check chapter 1.)

CANDLE COLOR: White. All purpose. (I happen to have plenty of plain tealights on hand.)

CRYSTAL OR STONES: Bloodstone and malachite for their healing energies. (See chapter 8.)

CHARM OR VERSE:

Icy garden rose of red and white, assist me now in my plight.

Sacred herbs of healing power, lend your magick in this hour.

Grant me recovery and good health, for it's back to work I go,

With a little help from a rose, healing rue, and the witch's yarrow.

SETUP: I already placed the rose and herbal foliage into a bud vase. I will place the vase next to my small cauldron. Inside of my cauldron is the tealight and the two stones for healing. I am placing these on top of the cast-iron, wood-burning stove in the living room. It is a safe place to let the candle burn inside of a small cauldron, as the cats stay off of there and my teenagers will know to leave it alone.

Cast a circle. Use a favorite quarter call, or use the "Circle of Trees."

Call the Goddess for her assistance:

Great Mother, I call on you. Help me to recover quickly from this illness.

Light the candle, say the verse three times.

Take a deep breath, close eyes, and imagine sinking roots into the ground the way a tree does. Visualize all fatigue, worry, or illness draining away and into the earth, where it will be absorbed harmlessly away. Now imagine healing energy coming back from the earth. It starts through the soles of the feet and then goes streaming up through all of the body. Raise up the arms and wiggle fingers. (I like to imagine that my fingers are like the leaves on the tree.) Feel stronger and happier. Lower arms. Take a deep breath and blow it out. Open eyes. Note: This is my version of what is called "grounding and centering."

Open the circle.

Allow the candle to burn out. Keep the flowers in the most-used room of the house (in my case, the living room).

See, that wasn't hard. It only took, from start to finish, about a half hour of my time. That includes writing the charm, gathering the supplies, and performing the spell. No muss. No fuss. I am a practical witch, after all. This is why you should know your basics, so when the time comes for magick, you simply step up and do the job.

You know, I really liked that spell. I think I'll call it the "Icy Rose Healing Spell." Now go and take the outline of this icy rose spell and the garden witch worksheet, and get to work. Apply this outline to the other herbal charms and spells in this book and those future garden witch spells of your own creation.

Start a new section in your garden witch Book of Shadows and title it "My Herbal Spells." Now come up with a few herbal spells and flower charms of your own. Don't let those blank pages scare you. Just think of all of the innovative garden magick that you can conjure up all by yourself. You can do it. I know you can.

Congratulations, You're a Garden Witch

We should stop for a moment and consider just what has brought us to this momentous occasion. Work, hard work; herbal study; experimentation; and the willingness to memorize basic spells and rituals, including those necessary astrological correspondence tables. You will try your hand at writing your own garden witch spells and will have consecrated or blessed your own sacred garden space.

We have tuned back in to nature and aligned ourselves to the wheel of the year by acknowledging and celebrating the changing seasons in all their glory. We have pondered the mysticism of trees, plants, and herbs, and awakened to the power of the elements. We've rediscovered the quiet sense of achievement that only a gardener can fully understand of breaking a sweat while working in the garden under a midday sun. We have enjoyed the mystery of the garden at night and the wonder of feeling the moonlight filter down on us through the leaves of the trees.

You have been rewarded with dirty knees and feet; red, ripe garden tomatoes and peppers; grubby hands, broken fingernails, and your first vase of magickal flowers from your own garden. How many sets of gardening gloves did you go through before you started disregarding them all together? You probably will have your gardening tools consecrated before too long. (I wonder what quarter the ceremonial garden hoe belongs to?) You decide. This book has enough information to keep you busy in the magickal garden for a good long while.

Though I do not believe that a plant will
spring up where no seed has been, I have great
faith in a seed. Convince me that you have a
seed planted there, and I am prepared
to expect wonders.

HENRY DAVID THOREAU

Final Thoughts

Just when you thought it was safe . . . another garden magick metaphor. Well, we certainly planted an awful lot of seeds, didn't we, with both new and old ways to look at nature and magick. Now that you have all these new and exciting ideas germinating in your mind, I can't wait to see what you will do with them. I *am* prepared to expect wonders from you. So get out there and get your hands in the soil. Plant those magickal herbs, trees, and flowers in the yard or in pots and containers. Make friends with new deities. Create your own garden witch spells and enchanting recipes!

The magickal path of the garden witch is an instinctive choice for those of us who sense the wonder and divinity of the natural world around us. Walk your chosen path wisely. Open your heart, tread gently, and see what you find.

By the shadow of the moon and light of the sun,

Happy gardening, blessed be, an' it harm none.

Millions of women . . . discover gardening.
Other people imagine that it is because
they have nothing better to do. In fact,
there is always something else to do,
as every woman who gardens knows.

GERMAINE GREER

Gardening Journal

Seasonal Quotations

January and February

> *The first fall of snow is not only an event;*
> *it is a magical event. You go to bed in one kind*
> *of world and wake up in another quite*
> *different, and if that is not enchantment*
> *then where is it to be found?*
>
> J. B. PRIESTLEY

2021 January - mid. In the 40's do good to get out in the sun - cold first thing then not so, then when sun starts to go down - <u>chilly</u>. Raked lots of leaves - didn't get to it in fall because of all the canning.

OK - real spring fever onset - 2 days weeding the rose garden in back. Restraint. Too early to prune them, but weeding and putting down layer of bark mulch (thanks Dad) and it looks so nice.

February 14 - LOTS of snow. 8" over a couple of days. Power & cable out because branch on east side pine broke & fell on the lines. Several other trees have broken limbs - so spring will be busy and may have to remove a tree or two or large parts of them.

> Winter is on my head, but
> eternal spring is in my heart.

VICTOR HUGO

Icicles I think are very underappreciated. Everyone knows the beauty of snowflakes — and of course they are, although whoever determined no two are alike was probably a dreamer. But sitting here at the dining room table watching snow, my eyes turn to the icicles. Whether or not they are all different, I think they are all unique. Plus they change — melt, freeze, melt, freeze any number of times before they are gone. Light through them and they sparkle. They've been blamed for injury to eyes and even a murder weapon in some creative who-done-its.

But what caught my eye was a bird hovering at the tip of the icicle outside this window. As the icicle started to melt and a drop of water formed, the bird waited as the water left the icicle and drank it. Here I am 74 and have never seen that amazing moment.

One kind word can warm three winter months.

JAPANESE PROVERB

208

March 12, 2021

The theme for this year (well one of them) is
"fertilize."

— Potting soil mix I'll try: equal parts
potting soil, manure and compost.
— banana under roses
— ZamZow's Thrive
1 gallon for center court
1 gallon for grapevines and pots
1 gallen for roses
1 gallen for SW garden

Snowbird Charm (Garden Charm for the Winter Months)

Work a charm for prosperity and peace this winter. At sunrise, draw a magickal symbol in the snow of your own choosing. Then make an offering to the birds of winter by filling up the bird feeder or sprinkling a bit of birdseed on the ground as you say this charm.

Snow that falls and icy winds that blow,

Come make this wintry spell of mine go!

Bring prosperity and peace, all year long,

Hear my call, as the birds welcome the dawn.

If we had no winter, the spring
would not be so pleasant . . .

ANNE BRADSTREET

March 21, 2020

This past week I've had window cleaner, fruit tree fertilizer and dormant spray (organic of course) and Dan started to prune sucker branches in the fruit trees. Spring ☺ On one of these wet, cold days I'd better do some inside spring cleaning.

March and April

> *Birds that cannot even sing–*
> *Dare to come again in Spring!*
>
> EDNA ST. VINCENT MILLAY

Spring comes: the flowers learn
their colored shapes.

MARIA KONOPRICKA

∾

∾ Spring is here! Clip some sunny daffodils from the garden and bring them inside to brighten your home.

Spring To-Do List

ॐ Rake off all of last year's fallen leaves. The hostas should start to break the ground any time now. Get those leaves off, so they can grow to the sun. Start watching for your earliest perennials, such as bleeding heart, columbine, and lily of the valley, to make their appearance.

ॐ Plant pansies now, they like the cold and their bright faces are sure to lift your spirits.

ॐ Fertilize your house plants and turn them to promote even growth.

ॐ Get your vegetable seeds and plant selections ready. Check and see when your local last frost date is.

Spring Seed Blessing Charm

Perform this on the night of a new moon.

Goddess bless these seeds, I hold the future in my hands,

Help them to grow and to bring beauty across the land.

May and June

Life is the flower for which love is the honey.

VICTOR HUGO

Arranging a bowl of flowers in the morning
can give a sense of quiet in a crowded day—
like writing a poem, or saying a prayer.

ANNE MORROW LINDBERGH

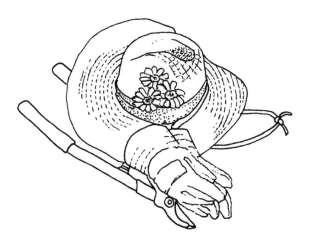

◌ Gather the yellow blossoms of the yarrow while it's looking its best. Coordinate the harvest with the appropriate phase of the moon, as was discussed in chapter 6. Hang the yarrow upside-down inside of a brown paper bag for a few weeks and allow it to air-dry. Then store the dried flowers in a nonporous, airtight container or old canning jar. Now you have an all-purpose magickal herb for your garden witchery and herbal spells for the rest of the year.

_____

_____

_____

_____

_____

_____

_____

_____

_____

_____

_____

_____

_____

_____

_____

_____

_____

_____

_____

_____

_____

_____

July and August

> *Flowers never emit so sweet and strong a*
> *fragrance as before a storm.*
> *When a storm approaches thee,*
> *be as fragrant as a sweet-smelling flower.*
>
> JEAN PAUL RICHTER

A garden always looks towards the future.

RITA BUCHANAN

❧ If you're looking to pump up the summer garden with some quick color, plant annuals. Use a little moon gardening magick and plant your annuals in the waxing moon.

❧ Remember to keep your gardens and your containers watered every day! Keep an eye on new trees and shrubs. Haul out your watering can or bucket and give the young trees a nice, deep drink.

September and October

> *Delicious autumn! My very soul is wedded to it, and if I were a bird I would fly about the earth seeking successive autumns.*
>
> GEORGE ELIOT

∾ This fall while you are planting bulbs for spring color, a good rule of thumb to follow is to plant the bulb two to three times deeper than the height of the bulb. If you are unsure of which end of the bulb is up, then lay the bulb on its side when you plant it. Even if you accidentally plant the bulb upside down, the shoots will instinctively grow up toward the sun.

∾ Try these shrubs for fantastic autumn color in your own garden:

Compact burning bush (*Euonymus campanulatus*), bright red, hardy to zone 4

Highbush blueberry (*Vaccinium corymbosum*), red, hardy to zone 3

European cranberry bush viburnum (*Viburnum opulus*), yellow to reddish purple, zone 3

Dwarf fothergilla (*Fothergilla gardenii*), yellow, scarlet, and orange, zone 5

November and December

At Christmas I no more desire a rose,
Than wish snow in May's newfangled mirth;
But like of each thing that in season grows.

WILLIAM SHAKESPEARE

ॐ Clip your roses back to about two thirds of their height to help them prepare for the winter months. If your rose bush stands at three feet tall, then clip about a foot of the canes back. Mulch the base of the bush with fallen leaves. Now your roses are all tucked in for winter.

ॐ This winter, don't cut back all of your withered foliage from your perennial garden. Leave it as it stands. It makes the garden more interesting in the winter months to see shapes under the snow or ice instead of a garden that's been whacked back to ground level. Also, the birds and animals will appreciate the cover and any leftover seeds for a snack.

ॐ Gather fresh holly and evergreen branches a week before Yule and use these for inexpensive natural holiday decorations. Arrange these on a mantle or shelf, add a few pillar candles, and you have a gorgeous natural decoration. (Make sure you keep the candle flames well away from the greenery.)

ॐ Try making your own centerpiece for the winter holidays. Start with Oasis, a green florist's foam, soaked in water, and cut the foam to fill your shallow container. Then arrange small branches of holly and ivy into the foam. You can make this diamond shaped or keep it circular. Now, fill in with other textures and varieties of evergreen. Try working with blue spruce, or fill in with clippings from the evergreen boxwood or add long-needled pine. If you live down South, try shiny rhododendron leaves or magnolia leaves. Insert a few red tapers securely into the center of your arrangement. Use green plastic candle cups and insert these into the foam. Add a bow or a few shiny red glass ornaments and have a happy holiday!

ॐ If the thought of floral design makes you too nervous, then simply tuck a few sprigs of berried holly around the base of a red candle and enjoy.

Every part of this earth is sacred . . . every shining pine needle, every sandy shore, every mist in the dark woods, every meadow, every humming insect. All are holy in the memory and experience of my people . . . We are part of the earth and it is part of us.

CHIEF SEATTLE, 1885

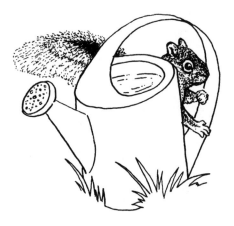

Glossary

ADVANCED PRACTITIONER: Comparable to a third-degree witch. A practitioner with many years of experience. A high priest or high priestess.

AMEND (soil): To amend is to add organic matter to your soil to improve it.

ANNUAL: A plant that completes its life cycle in one growing season.

BALEFIRE: A small ritual fire, usually contained in a cauldron.

BANISHING: Repelling an unwanted person or psychic entity.

BELTANE: One of the greater sabbats, Beltane begins at sundown on April 30. May 1 is Beltane Day or May Day.

BIENNIAL: A plant that grows vegetatively the first year and then is fruiting or dormant the second year. Foxglove and Queen Anne's lace are prime examples.

BONFIRE: A large outdoor fire.

BOOK OF SHADOWS: A witch's recipe/note book. A place to save all your various research. Often a witch's favorite charms and spells are listed as well.

BROWNIES: A benevolent, industrious earth elemental. Brownies are considered to be "house faeries"—see chapter 7.

CAULDRON: A large kettle, typically iron, with three legs. A witch's tool representing the element of water and a goddess symbol of regeneration and rebirth.

CHARM: A rhyming series of words (a spell) used for a specific magickal purpose.

CLAIRVOYANCE: The psychic ability to "see" or sense people, places, and events from the past, present, or future.

COVEN/CIRCLE: A group of Wiccans that worship and study together.

CUNNING MAN: An old term, traditionally meaning a male practitioner of magick and healing.

THE CRAFT: The witches' name for the Old Religion and practice of witchcraft.

DEAD-HEAD: To prune or pinch spent and withered foliage off a plant (not a follower of the band the Grateful Dead—that would be a Deadhead)!

DECIDUOUS: Trees, plants, and shrubs that shed their foliage in the fall and become dormant in the winter months.

DEOSIL: Moving in a clockwise direction for casting circles and to bring forth positive influences.

DIVINATION: The art and practice that seeks to foresee or foretell future events or hidden knowledge. Divination may be accomplished by psychic means or with the help of Tarot cards, scrying, or runes.

ELEMENTALS: Spirits or energies that coordinate with each element. Earth elementals are brownies and gnomes. Air elementals are faeries and sylphs. Water elementals are undines. Fire elementals are drakes, dragons, and djinns.

ELEMENTS: Earth, air, fire, and water.

ESBAT: A coven meeting or observance of a full moon.

ETHICS: If you don't know what these are, you are in a lot of trouble. See *Witches' Rede.*

FAERY: A nature spirit. Usually an earth or air elemental.

FASCINATION: The art of directing another's consciousness or will toward you. To command interest, to bewitch. Flower fascinations are covered in chapter 4.

FLORIGRAPHY: The language of flowers. See chapter 4.

GARDEN WITCH: A practical, down-to-earth type of practitioner. A witch who is well versed in herbal knowledge and its uses, and is a magickal gardener.

GREEN MAN: A well-liked, traditional interpretation of the God. Also, the Green Man sculpture is enjoying a current level of popularity as a garden ornament. The Green Man usually consists of a man's face surrounded by foliage and greenery.

GROUNDING AND CENTERING: A visualization technique. A way to focus and relax before or after performing magick. You push out negativity and stress from your own body, then you pull back into your body healthy and strong energy from the earth. (See chapter 10.)

HERBALISM: The use of herbs in conjunction with magick to bring about positive change.

HOLLY KING: The god of the waning year. His reign begins at the summer solstice and ends at the winter solstice.

IMBOLC: A Wiccan sabbat. A cross-quarter day and one of four greater sabbats traditionally celebrated on February 2. Also known as Brigid's Day, Candlemas, and Groundhog Day. The first spring festival.

INTERMEDIATE PRACTITIONER: Comparable to a second-degree witch, usually with three or more years of Craft experience under their belts.

KITCHEN WITCH: A hearth and home practitioner. One who celebrates and practices their craft in a quiet way using household tools and herbs.

LUGHNASADH: A greater sabbat that begins at sundown on July 31. Celebrated on August 1. The first of three harvest festivals, also known as Lammas.

MABON: The autumnal equinox and a Wiccan sabbat. The witches' Thanksgiving. Date changes year to year, from approximately September 21–23.

MAGICK: The combination of your own personal power used in harmony with natural objects such as crystals, herbs, and the elements.

MIDSUMMER: The summer solstice and a Wiccan sabbat. Midsummer is celebrated on or around June 21. This sabbat is also known as Litha. An opportune time to communicate with the faeries.

NATURAL MAGICIAN: A magician who works their magick mainly with the elements, in harmony with herbs and nature.

NOSEGAY: See *Posy.*

NOVICE: A beginner, a witch with less than a year's experience.

OAK KING: The god of the waxing year. His reign begins at the winter solstice, and he rules over the year until he is defeated by his brother, the Holly King, at Midsummer.

OSTARA: The vernal equinox and a Wiccan sabbat that falls on or around March 20. This is a spring celebration of the Goddess Eostre, and is a time to rejoice in life and new beginnings.

PERENNIAL: A perennial plant is one that lives three or more years. Herbaceous perennials are plants that are nonwoody, and whose above-ground parts usually die to the ground each winter. They survive the winter by means of their vigorous root systems.

POSY: An old term for a small, hand-held bouquet. Also known as a tussie-mussie and a nosegay.

SABBAT: One of eight solar festivals or holidays celebrated by Pagan religions, including Imbolc, Ostara, Beltane, Midsummer, Lughnasadh, Mabon, Samhain, and Yule. Often divided up as greater and lesser sabbats. The greater sabbats are Imbolc, Beltane, Lughnasadh, and Samhain. The lesser sabbats, Ostara, Midsummer, Mabon, and Yule, fall on the equinoxes and the solstices. A fast way to distinguish between the greater and the lesser sabbats is to realize that the dates of the greater sabbats never change. The solstices and equinoxes shift from year to year, depending on when the sun arrives into certain astrological signs.

SAMHAIN: Also known as Halloween, the witches' New Year. The day when the veil between our world and the spirit world is at its thinnest. This greater sabbat is celebrated on October 31. This popular holiday for children is also a time to honor the souls of loved ones who have passed, and is a time to celebrate the coming year.

SIMPLE: A simple is described as a medicinal plant. Also known as a basic element, having only one ingredient such as a flower or herb. See chapter 4.

SKYCLAD: Ritually naked.

TALISMAN: An object similar to an amulet. Designed for a specific magickal purpose.

TRIPLE MOON GODDESS: Refers to the three faces of the Goddess. The Maiden is symbolized by the waxing moon. The Mother is represented by the full moon, and the Crone is in sympathy with the waning moon. One example of such a trinity would be Artemis, Selene, and Hecate. See chapter 6.

TUSSIE-MUSSIE: A small bouquet. See *Posy*.

WICCA: The contemporary name for the religion of the witch. Wicca takes its roots from the Anglo-Saxon word *wicce*, which may mean "wise." It is also thought to mean "to shape or bend." A Pagan religion based on the cycles of nature and the belief in karma, reincarnation, and the worship of *both* a God and a Goddess.

WIDDERSHINS: Working in a counterclockwise (banishing) direction.

WISEWOMEN: The first witches and the custodians of the old herbal knowledge of benevolent spells and charms.

WITCHCRAFT: The craft of the witch.

WITCHES' REDE: The absolute rule that witches and magicians live by. The Rede states simply, "An' it harm none, do what ye will."

WITCHES' RUNE: A poem by Doreen Valiente. Doreen Valiente was considered to be "the mother of modern witchcraft." She wrote many of the traditional rituals and spells that modern witches hold near and dear to their hearts today, such as the poem version of "The Charge of the Goddess" and "The Witches' Rune" (below), a classic, all-purpose spell.

THE WITCHES' RUNE

Darksome night and shining Moon,

East, then South, then West, then North,

Harken to the Witches' Rune,

For here I stand to call you forth!

Earth and Water, Air and Fire,

Wand, Pentacle, and Sword,

Work you all to my desire,

Hark you now unto my word!

Cords and censor, scourge and knife,

Powers of the Witch's blade,

Wake you all now unto life,

Come now as the charm is made!

Queen of Heaven, Queen of Hel,

Horned Hunter of the Night,

Lend your power unto my spell,

Work my will by magic rite!

By all the power of Land and Sea,

By all the might of Moon and Sun,

As I do will, so mote it be!

Chant the spell and be it done!

WORT CUNNING: Herb craft.

YULE: The Wiccan sabbat celebrated on or around December 21. The winter solstice is the longest night and the shortest day. It is traditionally the time when Pagans celebrate the Mother Goddess and the return of the newly born Sun God. Decorated trees, the Yule log, fresh holly, mistletoe, and evergreen wreaths feature prominently in our decorations.

Bibliography

Adams, Anton and Mina. *The Learned Art of Witches and Wizards.* New York, N.Y.: Barnes and Noble Books, 2000.

Andrews, Ted. *Enchantment of the Faerie Realm.* St. Paul, Minn.: Llewellyn, 1993.

Bartlett, John. *Bartlett's Familiar Quotations,* 14th ed. Boston, Mass.: Little, Brown, and Company, 1968.

Bird, Richard. *Annuals.* New York, N.Y.: Lorenz Books, 1999.

Blakeney, E. H. *A Smaller Classical Dictionary.* Great Britain: Temple Press, 1934.

Brehmes, Lesley. *Complete Book of Herbs.* New York, N.Y.: Viking Studio Books, 1988.

Briggs, K. M. *The Fairies in English Tradition and Literature.* Chicago, Ill.: University of Chicago Press, 1967.

Budapest, Zsuzsanna. *The Grandmother of Time.* San Francisco, Calif.: Harper and Row, 1989.

Campanelli, Pauline. *Ancient Ways.* St. Paul, Minn.: Llewellyn, 1993.

Conway, D. J. *Moon Magick.* St. Paul, Minn.: Llewellyn, 1995.

———. *Maiden, Mother and Crone.* St. Paul, Minn.: Llewellyn, 1994.

———. *Magick of the Gods and Goddesses.* St. Paul, Minn.: Llewellyn, 1997.

Cunningham, Scott. *Cunningham's Encyclopedia of Crystal, Gem & Metal Magic.* St. Paul, Minn.: Llewellyn, 1992.

———. *Cunningham's Encyclopedia of Magical Herbs.* St. Paul, Minn.: Llewellyn, 1985.

———. *Magical Aromatherapy.* St. Paul, Minn.: Llewellyn, 1985 .

———. *Magical Herbalism.* St. Paul, Minn.: Llewellyn,1982.

Curran, Bob. *A Field Guide to Irish Fairies.* San Francisco, Calif.: Chronicle Books, 1988.

Cusick, Dawn. *The Book of Country Herbal Crafts.* Emmaus, Pa.: Rodale Press, 1991.

Dictionary of Quotations and Proverbs, The Everyman Edition. London, U.K.: Cathay Books, 1987.

Dunwich, Gerina. *The Pagan Book of Halloween.* New York, N.Y.: Penguin Compass, 2000.

Elliot, Charles. *The Quotable Gardener.* New York, N.Y.: The Lyons Press, 1999.

Fairies and Elves. The Enchanted World Series. Alexandria, Va.: Time-Life Books, 1984.

Farrar, Janet and Stewart. *The Witches' Way.* Custer, Wash.: Phoenix Publishing, 1984.

Ferguson, Diana. *The Magickal Year.* U.K.: Labyrinth Publishing, Ltd.,1996.

Friend, Rev. Hilderic. *Flowers and Flower Lore.* London, U.K.: Swan Sonnenschein and Co., 1884.

Gardening in the Shade. Des Moines, Iowa: Better Homes and Gardens Books, 1996.

Graves, Robert. *The White Goddess.* New York, N.Y.: Farrar, Straus, and Giroux, 1948.

Grounds for Gardening. University Extension, University of Missouri-Columbia, 1999. (Master Gardener reference guide.)

Guiley, Rosemary Ellen. *Encyclopedia of Witches and Witchcraft,* 2nd ed. New York, N.Y.: Checkmark Books, 1999.

Hendrickson, Robert. *Ladybugs, Tiger Lilies and Wallflowers, A Gardener's Book of Words.* New York, N.Y.: Prentice Hall, 1993.

James, Theodore Jr. *The Cut Flower Garden.* New York, N.Y.: McMillian Publishing Company, 1993.

Laufer, Geraldine Adamich. *Tussie-Mussies: The Victorian Art of Expressing Yourself in the Language of Flowers.* New York, N.Y.: Workman Publishing Company, 1993.

Loewer, Peter. *The Evening Garden.* New York, N.Y.: McMillan Publishing Company, 1993.

Manning, Al G. *Helping Yourself with White Witchcraft.* West Nyack, N.Y.: Parker Publishing Company, 1972.

Mercatantae, Anthony S. *The Magic Garden.* New York, N.Y.: Harper and Row, 1976.

Monaghan, Patricia. *The Book of Goddesses and Heroines.* St. Paul, Minn.: Llewellyn, 1990.

Murray, Elizabeth. *Cultivating Sacred Space, Gardening for the Soul.* San Francisco, Calif.: Pomegranate Publishing, 1997.

Nahmad, Claire. *Earth Magic.* Rochester, Vt.: Destiny Books, 1994.

———. *Garden Spells.* Philadelphia, Pa.: Running Press Books, 1994.

Quinn, Vernon. *Stories and Legends of Garden Flowers.* New York, N.Y.: Frederick A. Stokes Company, 1939.

Randolph, Vance. *Ozark Magic and Folklore.* New York, N.Y.: Dover Publications, 1947.

RavenWolf, Silver. *To Stir a Magick Cauldron.* St. Paul, Minn.: Llewellyn, 1995.

Riotte, Louise. *Sleeping with a Sunflower.* Pownal, Vt.: Gardenway Publishing, 1987.

Talbot, Rob, and Robin Whiteman. *Brother Cadfael's Herb Garden.* New York, N.Y.: Bulfinch Press Book, 1997.

Telesco, Patricia. *A Victorian Grimoire.* St. Paul, Minn.: Llewellyn, 1993.

Thiselton-Dyer, T. F. *The Folk-Lore of Plants.* London, U.K.: Chatto and Windus, Piccadilly, 1889.

Tyas, Robert. *The Language of Flowers or Floral Emblems.* London, U.K.: George, Routlage, and Sons, 1869.

Valiente, Doreen. *An ABC of Witchcraft, Past and Present.* Custer, Wash.: Phoenix Publishing, 1973.

———. *Natural Magic.* Custer, Wash.: Phoenix Publishing, 1975.

Walker, Barbra G. *The Woman's Dictionary of Symbols and Sacred Objects.* Edison, N.J.: Castle Books, 1988.

Wizards and Witches. The Enchanted World Series. Alexandria, Va.: Time-Life Books, 1984.

Wreaths and Other Nature Crafts: A Better Homes and Gardens Book. Des Moines, Iowa: Meredith Books, 1995.

Index